1. **Montacute House**
'The Skimmington Ride'
wall panel, hall c.1600

DECORATIVE PLASTERWORK

in the HOUSES *of* SOMERSET *1500 - 1700*

A REGIONAL SURVEY *by* JOHN *&* JANE PENOYRE
With a foreword by GEOFFREY BEARD

ACKNOWLEDGEMENTS

THE NATIONAL TRUST kindly allowed us to photograph in their houses, Montacute House, Lytes Cary and Dunster Castle.

Photographs:
Geoff Roberts: all colour photographs, and black & white photographs nos 2, 13, 14, 20, 29, 36, 37, 44, 49, 51, 59, 73, 81, 84, 85, 87, 89, 98, 100, 101, 114, 120, 121, 123
The Royal Commission on the Historical Monuments of England: nos 5, 33, 48, 116, and the frontispiece/cover photograph
The Victoria History of the County of Somerset: nos 39, 117
Gregory Penoyre: no 57, by courtesy of the Dean and Chapter of Westminster
Cecil and Kathleen French: no 18
Other photographs are by **John and Jane Penoyre**.

Drawings:
Distribution Maps and Chronological Table by **Peter Webb**
The drawing by Vredeman de Vries (fig. 7) is reproduced by courtesy of the **Board of Trustees of the Victoria and Albert Museum**.
W. Bidgood's drawing no 63 is reproduced from **SANHS Proceedings 1883**.
Line drawings are by **John Penoyre**.

Published by Somerset County Council 1994
Design and artwork by Peter Webb
Printed by Hammett & Co. Ltd., Taunton, Somerset
© John and Jane Penoyre 1993

ISBN 0 86183 265 5

CONTENTS

FOREWORD

by GEOFFREY BEARD M.A., D.Litt., F.S.A.

PLASTERWORK is anonymous stuff, rarely signed, and few plasterers' names appear in the conventional, or unconventional, literature of art history about it. Thus the attribution of plasterwork to particular craftsmen and dates is a more than usually hazardous task. It has to be made against too sketchy a framework, with appalling gaps in its structure, against the use of the same moulds and sources by many hands, and against the scant dependence of the plasterers on the usual pattern-books for their motifs. Patient research, such as that undertaken here, has to be based on extensive field-work. A pioneering start, in respect of Devon, had been made by the late Cecil French and his wife Kathleen. They did much to sort out the activities of the Abbott family of Frithelstock, to whom it has been fashionable of recent years to credit almost every south-west ceiling of note. It is therefore gratifying that the authors have given overdue credit to Robert Eaton, active at the end of Queen Elizabeth's reign, and probably responsible for work at Montacute House, Poundisford Lodge, West Coker, Combe Florey and Holcombe Court.

Regional surveys of plasterwork such as that now pubished here have, to my knowledge, only been undertaken for Hertfordshire and south Yorkshire. In all three cases it is patient comparison of like with like, the isolation of common motifs, the apparent use of the same moulds which push the subject forward, albeit slowly. Decorative plasterwork was created by skilled craftsmen, and for over four hundred years it has been an essential part of the interior decoration of the country house in Britain. Its frothy exuberance demands our attention and with its varied characteristics set out conveniently here it is possible to survey it all from the depth of the armchair and then plan to visit it in actuality. A small pair of binoculars will enhance the pleasure of the encounter, helping along the sense of wonder at the accomplishment and 'bravura' of it all.

Geoffrey Beard

AUTHORS' PREFACE

IN WRITING THIS BOOK and preparing it for publication we have had invaluable help from many people; but first we would like to thank all the householders who have so generously allowed us into their homes to draw, measure and photograph. We are most grateful for their interest, their kindness and their hospitality.

A study of this nature cannot be based altogether on original research and, although the field work is entirely our own, we are indebted for much of the background material to the writings of others, whose works are fully set out in the bibliography. In particular, we acknowledge in this regard the work of Geoffrey Beard, who has generously written the Foreword.

We are greatly indebted to Robert Dunning, editor of the Somerset *V.C.H.*, for his enthusiasm for the project, for giving us the benefit of his extensive knowledge of Somerset families and documents and for taking on the editing of the manuscript.

We are most grateful also to Somerset County Council and its Library Service who have undertaken the work of publishing, and in particular to Russell Lillford and Bob Croft of the council's Department for the Environment for their unfailing support and guidance throughout. Our thanks, too, to Peter Webb who has been responsible for the design and layout of the book, and to Geoff Roberts who has helped us by taking some of the more difficult black and white photographs and all the colour pictures.

Commander Desmond Williams, whose encyclopaedic knowledge of Somerset houses is legendary in the county, has introduced us to many buildings whose plasterwork might otherwise have remained unsuspected, as have Ron Gilson, Jenny Chesher and Michael McGarvie.

Jane Schofield, plasterwork conservator, and David Hayles of Hayles & Howe, plasterers, have both given us much needed help and advice on technique and conservation. Needless to say, any errors in that chapter will have stemmed from our incomprehension and not from any fault of theirs.

Kathleen French, who with her late husband Cecil French has made a pioneering and extensive study of the plasterwork of Devon, has kindly made available to us research notes and photographs.

Finally, our heartfelt gratitude for the generosity of all those, both private individuals and organisations, who have so splendidly contributed funds towards the cost of research and production. Without the generous sponsorship of the following, this study would never have seen the light of day:

- The Pilgrim Trust;
- The British Academy;
- The Maltwood Trust;
- Somerset & South Avon Vernacular Building Research Group;
- Mr & Mrs Simon Andrew;
- Mr & Mrs Keith Beers;
- Mr Roger Saul;
- Mr & Mrs Robert Vaux;
- Mr Ralph Vivian-Neal.

Minehead

Bridgwater

Glastonbury

Frome

AVON

WILTS

Taunton

Yeovil

DEVON

Chard

DORSET

DISTRIBUTION MAP

INTRODUCTION

HOUSES AND COTTAGES in South-West England, particularly in Devon and Somerset, are rich in decorative plasterwork. Contemporary houses in other regions, notably in the West Midlands, the Pennines, East Anglia or South-East England, are often more elaborately constructed than the essentially simple buildings of the South-West, but few can boast such a wealth of interior decoration. In Somerset (the post-1974 county excluding Avon) houses containing decorative plasterwork are unevenly distributed. They lie thick on the ground in the rich Vale of Taunton, in all the countryside around the Quantock hills and in much of the southern part of the county. Further west into Exmoor, in the central Levels and on the Mendips there are few examples, but there are many around Frome and Beckington, an area that owed its considerable wealth to the woollen cloth industry.

The use of plaster as an easily moulded decorative medium was first introduced into England from Italy during the reign of Henry VIII and can be regarded as a renaissance phenomenon in this country. The period 1500-1700 was one of headlong fundamental change from medieval ways of thought and expression in art and architecture to the new classical rationalism based on the study of the writings and buildings of ancient Rome. The interest and excitement of the period, the speed of development and the strange by-ways that bedevilled architecture on its course towards the full expression of ordered classical design make this one of the most romantic and fascinating periods in the history of the visual arts.

In England, far away from Italy where the Renaissance originated, the new age came late, but by the middle of the sixteenth century it was evoking a response. It might be expected that a similar time-lag in the adoption of new fashions would exist between Court circles around London and the South-West provinces, but the actual difference between contemporary design there and the more sophisticated South-East is hardly apparent. New fashions spread fast within the country because of the enthusiasm, in those changing times, for being up to date. This tendency in the West owed much to one of the most powerful magnates in the country, Edward Seymour, duke of Somerset, whose protegees at Court built such trend-setting and influential houses as Lacock Abbey and Longleat.[1]

Medieval building techniques, however, were only gradually abandoned and Italian-inspired architectural designs only tentatively tried out as decoration in such isolated features as doorways, fireplaces, tombs and internal plasterwork where the new ideas could, so to speak, do no harm. Later Elizabethan and Jacobean architecture, coloured by Flemish taste, gave way towards the mid seventeenth century to a purer classical style following Inigo Jones's influential designs for the Court.[2] The style of decoration in plasterwork mirrors the course of these changes, starting in the earlier schemes with echoes of the fifteenth century Perpendicular style and ending, during the last part of the seventeenth century, in the full-blown expression of ordered classicism.

Plaster, a mixture of lime and sand variously reinforced with organic material, has been used as a wall covering certainly since Saxon times in this country, usually to cover up rough stonework or as a base for painted decoration. Gypsum makes the finest plaster and was used in England in the thirteenth century from material quarried in Montmartre - hence the name Plaster of Paris. In the seventeenth century deposits of gypsum in the form of alabaster were quarried around Watchet,[3] and were extensively used for sculpture[4] and presumably for making plaster for fine internal work.

The idea of using the material decoratively originated from the Italian technique of moulding in high relief in plaster (*stucco* in Italian) or in the superior hard plaster made from Travertine (*stucco duro*). Henry VIII when he was building his new palace of Nonsuch in the 1530s employed Italian craftsmen to decorate the outside walls with classical motifs, heraldic emblems and mythological figures, all in high relief in *stucco duro*. This is the first use of the technique in England of which there is certain knowledge.[5] The palace was demolished at the end of the seventeenth century and only one or two fragments of the decoration survive. Far away in Derbyshire the famous overmantels and wall decorations in Hardwick Old Hall were also made of this material and have survived in the unfinished ruins, exposed to the open air since the project was abandoned half-built in 1590, a remarkable tribute to the quality of both plaster and workmanship. But *stucco duro* never became popular in England, presumably because of the difficulty and expense in obtaining the proper materials.

Decorative plasterwork in the South West is all internal; there is virtually no external pargetting or decorative render at all. Many small buildings in Somerset, and some quite large ones in Devon, are built of cob (compacted clay) and plastered outside as a protection, but these houses have never been given moulded plaster decorations on their walls like the wholehearted pargetting of East Anglian timber buildings.

2. **Court House, East Quantoxhead**.
Overmantel in Hall with the Luttrell coat of arms and the date, 1629

Plasterwork in the area is to be found principally in ceilings, overmantels and friezes. From earliest times the hearth had been the central focus of the house and when in the sixteenth century chimneys were introduced, the chimney-piece and its overmantel were given pride of place as the centre for decorative display. It is here that the owner showed off his wealth and lineage with lavish achievements of arms *(fig. 2)* or with biblical or classical scenes, all in elaborately decorated surrounds or, more simply, with the initials of himself and his wife and, perhaps, a date.

The frieze, a strip of decoration around the room at high level between the panelling or wall hanging and the ceiling, was sometimes made in timber as part of the panelling but far more often in plaster. It is in the frieze that designs are most interesting, more elaborate than those in the ceilings, less flamboyant than those in the overmantels. Here classical motifs, often repetitive, form flowing patterns including mythological beasts, shields of arms, animals and plants, all represented in seemingly infinite variety. These three elements of ceiling, frieze and overmantel are treated separately in later chapters.

Inventiveness and love of decoration are obvious characteristics of the sixteenth and seventeenth centuries in England. Elizabethan and Jacobean clothes are lavishly patterned and embroidered and both jewellery and furniture are notable for elaboration of design. All available surfaces are smothered in decoration and there can scarcely be a chest or a chair of any quality, a pew-end or bedstead that is not carved all over with fanciful patterns. As with panelling and furniture, so with the cheaper and more easily-worked plaster which presented a splendid opportunity for lavish designs on ceilings, walls and fireplaces.

Decorative plasterwork in varying degrees of elaboration is found in the houses of a wide social range in Somerset, from mansions to small farmhouses, the latter often decorated with a surprising richness and skill, although in some cases the designs are naive and primitive. Even in what today are classed as cottages, fragments of decoration can sometimes be found, half concealed behind a modern staircase or hung with dark cobwebs above an inserted bedroom ceiling, reminders of the fluctuating fortunes of the agricultural community.

Most of the plasterwork in rural England is the work of native craftsmen. In the more ambitious schemes they derived their designs from pattern books. Many of these were printed abroad and were the principal means of importing foreign ideas of decoration. Foreign craftsmen, either deliberately invited as the French and Italians were in the early sixteenth century, or refugees from oppression like the later Flemish immigrants, were few in number compared with the enormous volume of work executed. They may have, and probably did, set the pace in so far as examples of their work could be admired and copied, and in seaports such as Barnstaple, Dartmouth and Bristol, with a constant flow of foreign traffic, a few examples of what is almost certainly Flemish work of the late sixteenth or early seventeenth centuries can be seen.

The amount of work surviving from the sixteenth century, considerable though it is, is far less than that from the seventeenth century and covers a different range of styles. The earlier work comprises designs of Italian and later of Flemish origin in friezes and overmantels and of medieval origins in ceilings. Designs of the seventeenth century range through all the vicissitudes of Flemish- and German-inspired decoration until the fully-developed classical style emerges during the latter half of the century.

Plasterwork in the eighteenth century loses its regional character and becomes more stereotyped in design, retaining little of the inventiveness of the earlier work. There is no longer anything so dramatic as the emergence of the full Renaissance. Rather, designs are limited to refinements and variations of the classical idiom based on a universal acceptance of style which left a good deal less room for individuality. This study therefore goes no further than around 1700 and is confined to the more historically interesting and visually dramatic work of the preceding two hundred years.

---

1 Edward Seymour, Lord Protector 1546-50; built Somerset House, London, *c*.1540. Laycock Abbey, Wilts., built by William Sharington, a friend of the duke, 1540-50; Longleat, built by Sir John Thynne, the duke's surveyor of works, 1547-70.

2 Inigo Jones (1573-1652), Surveyor of the King's Works, architect of the Banqueting House, Whitehall, 1621.

3 *V(ictoria) C(ounty) H(istory) of Somerset*, ii, 354-5; ibid. v, 145

4 Eg. fonts at Elworthy and Williton: *V.C.H. Somerset*, v. 73, 168

5 G. Beard, *Decorative Plasterwork in Great Britain*, 25

**3. Poundisford Park,
Pitminster**
*The Hall, c.1570;
an early ceiling
with pendants*

CHAPTER 1

SOURCES, STYLE *and* SYMBOLISM

THE PATTERNS THAT DECORATE the plaster ceilings, friezes and overmantels in sixteenth century houses are derived from two sources. Firstly they come from medieval forms - in the case of ceilings from the fan-vaults of late medieval buildings such as Henry VII's chapel at Westminster Abbey; and secondly from the complicated naturalistic designs from fifteenth century Italy, with their reference back to the patterns of ancient Rome. It is this fusing of the two very different cultures that gives to so much early renaissance design in England its charm and vitality.

All European medieval craftsmen, not least the English, had a love of inventing strange dragons and other mythical beasts which formed so strong an element in their carvings and illuminations. Such creatures also occur in ancient Roman work and in renaissance designs, the latter changing from the gothic to the classic mode and recognisably of mixed Roman and gothic ancestry. Such fancifully designed monsters form an important element in much English plasterwork of the sixteenth and early seventeenth centuries. They most often occur in friezes, their ferocious heads sprouting foliage and their bodies trailing off into flowing scrolly patterns of leaves, fruit and flowers *(fig. 4)*.

All renaissance designers looked to Italy for their inspiration, albeit in England at second or third hand. The enquiring, rational and scientific approach to life that was sweeping through Europe, coupled with the realisation of what so very long ago had been achieved by the ancient Romans, induced a boundless enthusiasm among the better educated for all things Roman. By the year 1500 the great upsurge of intellectual and artistic activity which had been going on in Italy for a hundred years and more had already made itelf felt in France, where Italian ideas of art and architectural decoration were becoming fashionable.

Throughout the fifteenth century, during which the Renaissance had blossomed in Italy, England, insular, geographically remote and preoccupied with her own dynastic struggles, had hardly taken part in that great movement in so far as the visual arts were concerned. The time-lag that consequently existed between England and Italy is dramatically illustrated by the magnificent Perpendicular church towers of Somerset, some of which were erected as late as the 1540s. Such essentially gothic structures, unsurpassed examples of late-medieval architecture, are actually coeval with works of the Italian High Renaissance like Michelangelo's Medici Chapel in Florence, completed in 1523, while Brunelleschi's Pazzi Chapel, which signals the start of the architectural renaissance in Florence, had been built a hundred years earlier still.

In Italy, although ancient Roman structural achievement and building technique were evident in the remains still standing above ground, less was known of Roman interior decorative style. Consequently, enormous enthusiasm was shown when in 1488, under the influence of the archaeologically-inclined Cardinal Giovanni dei Medici, decorative stucco reliefs and wall paintings of the Augustan period were discovered in the vaults below the Baths of Trajan, thought at the time to have been the 'Golden House of Nero'.[6] This often quoted story is worth repeating because it marks the starting point of so much renaissance

4. Three Winged Monsters

Roman. *Painted wall decoration from the Augustan period*

Late medieval. *Fifteenth century wood carving from the church at Llananno, Powis*

Renaissance. *Late sixteenth century plaster frieze from Holcombe Court, Holcombe Rogus, Devon*

decoration. The schemes thus revealed were as striking as the technique, comprising painted and stucco designs on walls and ceilings laid out in symmetrical patterns. The motifs included attenuated architectural forms combined with naturalistic trailing plants, candelabra, vases, naked and partly clothed figures and fabulous animals. The underground cave-like vaults were called in Italian *grotti* and hence the style became known as *grotesche* or, as we say today, grotesque. In 1517 Raphael was commissioned to decorate the Loggia, a huge arcaded gallery in the Vatican, with designs based on the grotesque, and his work was much admired and copied.

Grotesque design ideas were adopted all over Europe, first in France where Francis I was experimenting with the new forms in his palaces at Fontainbleau and on the Loire (*c*.1520-30), then in the Low Countries and in England, coming to us first via Italian and French craftsmen working for the Court. At much the same time the spread of these ideas was encouraged by the publication of numerous treatises and pattern books. Sebastiano Serlio's *Architettura*[7] was one of the early works of this type and contains towards the end of the fourth book, first published in Venice in 1537, many designs and decorative schemes including ceilings in the grotesque manner, in detail very like one installed in Hampton Court for Cardinal Wolsey fifteen or so years before *(fig. 5)*.

5. *The ceiling of* **Wolsey's Closet**, **Hampton Court**, *installed by Venetian craftsmen c.1520*

There was no great upsurge of building activity in England until the reign of Henry VIII when he and Wolsey embarked on a policy of extravagant palace building both for their own aggrandisement and as a bid to put the country on an equal footing with its rival, France. In their huge palaces, Hampton Court and Nonsuch, they employed Italian craftsmen as Henry had already done when in 1512 he engaged Pietro Torrigiano for the design and construction of his father's tomb in Westminster Abbey. Wolsey employed Venetian craftsmen who were responsible for the terracotta roundels containing busts of Roman emperors which decorate the exterior of Hampton Court as well as for the interior decoration (more particularly, for the purpose of tracing the history of ceiling design, the ceiling of the small room called Wolsey's Closet, completed shortly before 1525 when Henry took over the palace).

By the late 1530s, following the king's break with Rome, England's contact with Italy was considerably curtailed. Italian craftsmen were no longer welcome nor were they prepared to risk their reputations by working in heretic England. France, too, was shunned as a Catholic country, although not to the same extent. Thus by the mid century England was looking elsewhere for inspiration, to the Low Countries and to Germany, particularly to Flanders with whom she had close trade relations. Things Flemish and German became fashionable and Flemish and German craftsmen and their pattern books were widely used, introducing their own version of the grotesque, virtually a new style of decoration *(fig. 6)*. The printing presses of northern Europe were at this time in full production, notably that of Christophe Plantin in Antwerp,[8] and books, which had previously been rare, hand-crafted treasures became freely available.

As the architectural and decorative schemes of ancient Rome were adopted, each country modified the style in the light of its particular national genius. First the Italians, in the buildings of the early Renaissance, gave the formalised Roman designs a fresher and more restrained aesthetic; then the French adapted the Italian decorations to conform to their own ideas of purity of form and elegance; while the Flemish and German designers gave the Italian grotesque a northern European flavour with a pronounced leaning towards exaggeration and the macabre, much in the tradition of such late-medieval painters as Hieronymous Bosch. Their designs were in spirit quite different from the freshness and grace of the Italian and French work. Hans Vredeman de Vries from Antwerp and Wendel Dietterlin from Germany were two foreign writers published towards the end of the sixteenth century. These two authors, particularly Vredeman, were extremely influential, their works crammed with an amazing wealth of detailed designs. They were consummate draughtsmen and produced the most sophisticated schemes using cleverly distorted classical elements, an extreme aspect of what has come to be called Mannerism, and in the case of Dietterlin with a deliberate emphasis on the sinister and even the satanic.

In less sophisticated English hands, or in Flemish hands under English skies, the spirit of the designs was again transformed by the elimination of the grosser features, so little of the Flemish spooky flavour came through. There was, however, one element in Flemish mannerist design which appealed universally to English taste, that of strapwork *(fig. 7)*.

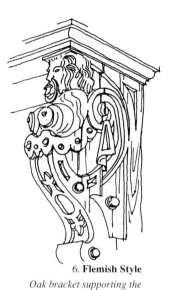

6. Flemish Style
Oak bracket supporting the jetty of a house in Dartmouth

7. Strapwork on Overmantels in the **Court House, East Quantoxhead** *c.1620 and* **Poundisford Lodge, Pitminster**, *1590, compared to a drawing by Vredeman de Vries, published in 1581*

Strapwork, the framework and background to much late sixteenth- and early seventeenth-century design in northern Europe, had been only a minor element in the Italian and French designers' vocabulary and had not been allowed to dominate. In Flemish hands it assumed paramount importance, becoming more and more fanciful and complicated and was adopted here in Elizabethan and Jacobean times to become the flavour of the period. Strapwork, a good descriptive term, comprises patterns in plaster, stone or wood, of inter-weaving flat straps in imitation of leather *(fig. 8)*. The straps, frequently studded or pierced, are combined with fantastically-shaped flat plates which as often as not curl up at the

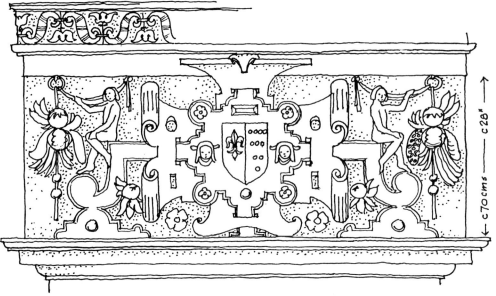

8. West Coker Manor House
Overmantel, c.1600; an example of early seventeenth century strapwork

edges and project as wings or are rolled into decorative batons. Strapwork will be mentioned in later chapters, sometimes found in friezes, seldom in ceilings, but almost always in the showy overmantels of the period.

Of the English pattern books, **A Booke of Sundry Draughts** by Walter Gedde, published in 1615, was undoubtedly used as inspiration for the design of later ceiling frets. His book was specifically for the use of 'glaziers and plaisterers' and an example of a ceiling at Nutcombe Manor, Devon *(fig. 61)*, is shown alongside the illustration in Gedde's book from which the design was taken *(fig. 62)*.

The style most frequently adopted in plaster friezes from the mid sixteenth century was a form of grotesque referred to at the time as the 'antike', 'antique' or 'antic'. Essentially, the style took the Roman grotesque motifs - vases, candelabra, putti, dolphins, sphinxes and strange animals - and wove them into densely packed foliage arranged in flowing scrolls. Monsters' heads, animals and plants are indistinguishable; bodies change into tendrils, heads sprout leafy crests and all are elegantly arranged in flowing patterns. The earliest example of the style in or near Somerset known to the writers is not in plaster but in carved stone, high up under the battlements of Abbot Chard's porch at Forde Abbey, Dorset *(fig. 9)*. The porch, built *c*.1530, is a late-medieval structure in the sixteenth-century Perpendicular style complete with traceried and mullioned windows and the frieze, which has sphinxes, vases and other antike motifs showing all the assurance of Italian design, sits oddly over the corner buttress shafts and tracery below.

9. Renaissance Carving
Stern faced Sphinxes on the porch at Forde Abbey, Dorset, c.1520

There had developed during the sixteenth and early seventeenth centuries a craze for symbolism, for punning, for hidden meanings and obscure ironical jokes and what the Elizabethans called 'devices'. Such ideas were incorporated in all sorts of designs, in coats of arms, in carvings and in plasterwork decorations throughout the country. There are, for example, roses entwined with thistles, representing at first sight the combined thrones of England and Scotland under James I. But there is a hidden meaning: thistles are for marital fidelity and roses for the transience of human life (the petals fade and fall), both considered appropriate embellishments for a matrimonial chamber. Other such symbolism can be found in many decorative schemes. Distinguishing emblems were used to identify the various symbolical personalities which occur as the centrepiece of a ceiling or, more often, as flanking figures on either side of an overmantel - identified by such emblems as an olive branch for Peace, an anchor for Hope, a cornucopia for Plenty (suitable for a dining room) and scales for Justice (perhaps to suggest the owner's role as lord of the manor or justice of the peace). All such symbolism was fully understood by an educated visitor.

One of the most frequently found motifs is the dolphin. The use of this attractive creature in decoration has a long history. It can be seen on ancient Greek pottery and on Roman works of all kinds - mosaics, silverware, even tombstones. In medieval Europe it was the symbol of the Dauphin of France and in Elizabethan England, apart from its obviously decorative quality, it stood for Affection. The origin and meaning of the Tudor rose is too well known to need description, as are the Homeric origins of that other favourite, the mermaid (Worldly Enticement). But the fleur-de-lis, which enjoyed a very long period of popularity and was used from our earliest plasterwork examples at least until the end of the seventeenth century, deserves a mention. Originally thought of as symbolising the Virgin Mary, plain fleurs-de-lis can be seen in medieval churches throughout Europe. Louis VII of France took it for the royal coat of arms in the 12th century and the Venetians in their use of it split the centre lobe and filled it with seeds, the form most often seen in English plasterwork - more like an iris than a lily *(fig. 10)*.

10. *Four* **Fleurs de lis**, *from the heraldic type to the floral flourish of the early eighteenth century. From left to right:* **Lytes Cary** *c.1530;* **Orchard Wyndham** *c.1540;* **Forsters, Shapwick** *1712;* **Beckington Abbey** *c.1640 and* **Mapperton, Dorset** *c.1550*

During the late Elizabethan and Jacobean period designs became more and more fanciful and ornate until, with the revelations of renewed travel to Italy which had once again become feasible in Stuart times, the nation-wide adoption of what had by then become true classical design took its place. Symbolism, using classical rather than medieval or heraldic emblems and motifs, continued in importance, so dolphins and mermaids still abound but Tudor roses disappear. Fleurs-de-lis, however, although medieval in origin, were still used; perhaps they owed some popularity to their continuing use in the royal coat of arms. The motifs of ancient Rome were adopted more or less without change; the wreath of laurel or bay, the palm-leaf fronds, the garlanded ox-skull, the swags of cloth and garlands of fruit and flowers, and the ever present putti or amorini climbing amongst the foliage of the acanthus scrolls, all appeared in their fully developed form in the new architecture.

The one Italianate feature that above all appealed to the late Stuart plasterers was the ceiling wreath. Inigo Jones had used a huge oval as the dominant feature of the timber ceiling of the Banqueting House in Whitehall (completed in 1622). In this dramatic and influential building, gone was any hint of strapwork, of fan-vault inspired patterns or of grotesques. Here was a ceiling that looked straight to the gods with, between the deep beams and inside the great oval, painted pictures by Peter Paul Rubens demonstrating all the sophisticated expertise of Baroque perspective. Fruit and flowers, acanthus scrolls and fully developed cornices with modillion brackets all in high relief became, as it were overnight, the only style of decoration worth having in great houses.

11. Coalharbour Farm, Ham, Creech St. Michael

Parlour ceiling; an oval wreath of the mid seventeenth century

It took only a little while for the new ideas adopted by the Court and the aristocracy to percolate down the social layers. By the second half of the seventeenth century the classical idiom had been accepted in even quite small houses, classical cornice mouldings and ceiling wreaths becoming almost universal *(fig. 11)*. Overmantels were now supported on or framed by wide plaster acanthus-leaved brackets and friezes were formed of monotonously-repeated swags and garlands.

Towards the end of the seventeenth century this ponderous classicism was becoming less solemn and by around 1700 the style had been modified by the introduction of lighter and more naturalistic designs, in contrast with the solid laurels and bays of the mid century. By the middle of the eighteenth century this refinement had developed into the well known and exaggeratedly delicate Adam style, based on the then recent discoveries of the wall paintings in the ruins of ancient Pompeii. By that time individual contributions by local craftsmen had become less important than the detailed and specific instructions of the architect and his learned patron.

MOTIFS AND SYMBOLS

Motifs and symbolism typical of sixteenth- and seventeenth-century plasterwork designs

Anchor . . . . Hope

Book . . . . Wisdom

Cornucopia . . . . . . Plenty

Dolphin . . . . Affection (the Dauphin of France)

Fleur-de-lis . . . . . . Royal arms of France

Ivy . . . . Friendship, drinking (Dionysus, Bacchus)

Lamb . . . . Mercy

Laurel or Bay . . . . . Victory, Art

Mermaid . . . . Worldly enticement

Moon . . . . Empire

Oak leaves . . . . Strength, Power

Palm . . . . Martyrdom, Peace

Peacock . . . . Immortality

Pegasus , ... Triumph of Good over Evil

Phoenix . . . . Resurrection; emblem of Elizabeth I

Pineapple . . . . Fertility

Pomegranate . . . . . Emblem of Catherine of Aragon, later used decoratively

Portcullis . . . . Emblem of Henry VIII

Roses . . . . Transience of earthly life

Serpent . . . . Wisdom

Scales . . . . Justice

Sword . . . . Justice

Thistle . . . . Marital Fidelity

Tudor rose . . . . Emblem of Tudors

Vine . . . . Eternal Love, Friendship

6 Beard, *Decorative Plasterwork*, 23

7 Sebastiano Serlio, *The Five Books of Architecture*.

8 Such books are displayed at the Plantin-Moretus Museum, Antwerp.

**12. Lytes Cary,
Charlton Mackerell**
*Great Chamber, c.1533;
an early Tudor ceiling*

CHAPTER 2

CEILINGS

*Further illustrations
are on pages 54 to 61*

IN THE SECOND HALF of the sixteenth century the new form of ceiling decoration came into general use throughout the country. The Hall, the most important room in the house, had until the early years of the sixteenth century been open to the roof, the elaborate display of timbers, smoke-blackened from the open hearth, making an impressive if sombre climax to the interior. Tudor improvements included the replacement of the open hearth with an enclosed fireplace and the flooring over of the open hall to make more chambers. The resulting flat-ceiled halls were built at a little above the normal storey height in small houses and a whole two storeys high in the larger houses to emphasise their importance.

At first the flat ceilings were made of heavy moulded beams and exposed floor joists. Such timber ceilings were dark and oppressive in spite of the early Tudor practice of painting designs on the beams and the spaces between the joists. Even Cardinal Wolsey's flat timber ceiling in his Closet or private study in Hampton Court, ostentatiously opulent though it was with intricate Italianate patterns and plenty of gold leaf, could not add much reflected light to the sombre Tudor interior.

The use of plaster to make a continuous surface to a ceiling was an innovation that came about at the same time as the fashion for much larger windows. Such ceilings, white and flat, were in total contrast to the dark timber ceilings of the past. The opportunity for decoration that they presented was eagerly grasped and the essentially mouldable nature of plaster led to elaborate patterns in relief, known as 'frets', the moulded ribs picking up the light from the big windows, the whole effect heightened by the glitter of refracted light from the multitude of tiny panes.

These flat white plaster ceilings, richly embroidered with fine lines of ribbing and patterned with small emblems, typical of Elizabethan work, appear to be unique to the British Isles, other European countries continuing to use heavy beams and painted decoration until the introduction of classical designs.

But not all ceilings are flat. Some upper chambers still retain the shape of the roof structure above, resulting in barrel-shaped or three-sided, tunnel-like ceilings. For convenience all such concave ceilings are referred to generally as 'barrel' ceilings, including the somewhat later segmentally curved ones.

The designs of plasterwork ceilings are enormously varied and reveal endless combinations of complicated patterns but, by comparing a number of examples, it is possible to suggest a progression of characteristics in roughly chronological sequence. Ceilings are very rarely dated; overmantels often are but were not necessarily put in at the same time as the ceilings. Where coats of arms are incorporated in the decorative scheme, commemorating marriages or other notable events, the ceilings can sometimes be dated with a fair degree of certainty and, by stylistic comparison with those dated examples, an estimate of period can be made of the others.

13. **Gaulden Manor, Tolland**
detail from hall ceiling, c.1640;
King David

SINGLE-RIB CEILINGS, *c.*1530-1600

The earliest plaster ceilings have thin single ribs forming the patterns, at first in straight lines following more familiar joinery techniques. Around 1500 late Perpendicular church roofs of the West Country, low pitched and richly decorated, were often panelled in squares and rectangles with timber bosses and carved leaves at the intersections of the ribs. That these characteristics should at first be carried over into the new material is only to be expected. The ceiling of Wolsey's Closet was also made of wood, with little lead leaves and bosses to cover the joints between the ribs. Made by Italian workmen, the densely packed pattern of straight ribs was arranged in octagons and squares, like the pattern of the coffered vaults of ancient Rome. (Such 'Roman' designs were to be illustrated by Serlio in his fourth book, published in 1537).[9] The pattern of the Solar ceiling in **Orchard Wyndham, Williton** may be based on the Hampton Court design using plaster instead of wood and lead, the rib intersections covered with a plaster leaf or boss. The only other decoration in early plaster ceilings were isolated motifs in the panels between the ribs. These took the form of crests, Tudor roses, fleurs-de-lis or perhaps a shield of arms, all derived from medieval decoration. Motifs derived from Italian sources were at first confined to friezes.

Early ceiling patterns are small in scale, the whole ceiling closely patterned like the oriental carpets that were fashionable at the time. Towards the end of the sixteenth century patterns begin to open out, spaces between the ribs becoming larger, giving a lighter and more airy effect *(fig. 55)*.

The Great Chamber at **Lytes Cary, Charlton Mackrell** is the first plaster ceiling in the county known to the writers comprising a simple but densely-packed stellar pattern covering the three sides of a barrel, the only motifs used being fleurs-de-lis and small shields *(fig. 12)*. In the lunette or trapezoid shape where the ceiling joins the wall at the end of the room there is a royal shield of arms of Henry VIII flanked by Tudor roses and fleurs-de-lis. The Chamber is part of the south-west wing added by John Lyte to the medieval hall range in 1533 (the date is carved on the outside of the bay window) and the shields of arms on the ceiling and bay window show the Lyte and Horsey arms, relating to John's marriage to Edith Horsey some years before. This is an early example of a stellar pattern which developed to its full splendour in late Elizabethan times. Very nearly contemporary is the flat Solar ceiling at **Orchard Wyndham**, referred to above *(fig. 14)*. Here the geometric pattern, still of straight ribs, incorporates large fleurs-de-lis and leaf bosses and, in the centre of each panel, a badge with the arms of Wyndham and Sydenham (marriage 1528).[10] It seems likely that the ceiling was erected some time after this date, perhaps when John Wyndham was knighted in 1547, the later date being more appropriate to the style of the design.

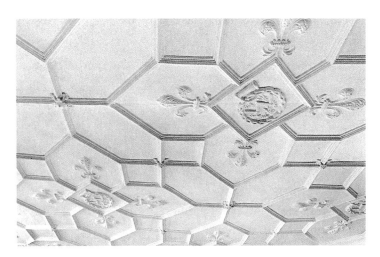

14. **Orchard Wyndham,
Williton**. *Solar ceiling, c.1550*

As craftsmen became more familiar with their plastic material, designs which included curves became popular, curves in the horizontal plane making leaf and petal shapes and in the vertical sense as the ribs curve down to pendants. Pendants are features of late Perpendicular fan-vaulted roofs, the culminating expression of English medieval architecture and the other main inspiration for these decorative schemes.[11] Thus many sixteenth-century ceilings emulate fan vaults with curving profiles and hanging pendants, the plaster ribs gathering together at the nodal points of the design and swooping down to pendants or wall corbels. Excellent examples of the style may be seen in the Hall at **Poundisford Park, Pitminster** *(fig. 59)* and in the Great Chamber at **Mapperton** in Dorset *(fig. 56)*. These ceilings spring from a grotesque frieze which in both cases is bracketed out on a deeply coved cornice, making the patterned ceiling and its pendants float free of the walls like a flat canopy.

The tall, elegant Hall in **Poundisford Park** *(fig. 3)* was built by a Taunton merchant, William Hill, *c.*1546 but his initials and those of his second wife Lucy Ryves appear on two of the pendants and their marriage around 1570 dates the ceiling to then or soon after unless, of course, the initials were additions to older plasterwork.[12] A date *c.*1550 seems likely for the ceiling at Mapperton.

In the ceiling of the upper chamber of the **Gatehouse, Combe Florey**, although the pattern of the ribs is very similar to the two examples quoted above, there are no pendants. The room has a fine overmantel dated 1593, a realistic enough date for the ceiling which has an unusual distinguishing feature, a ring of very small faces looking like masks surrounding the bosses at the intersections. Two other houses have similar face-masks, **Newton Surmaville, Barwick** *(fig. 102)*, and the Court Room at **Holcombe Court, Holcombe Rogus**, Devon. Both houses have stellar patterned ceilings but all the ribs in the Holcombe Court ceiling are curved, making a pattern of interlocking petals rather than straight-sided stars. This ceiling is associated with a overmantel dated 1591.

During the latter half of the sixteenth century a new decorative feature appeared, the floral spray. Used in the spaces between ceiling ribs, at first the device comprised a tight bunch of leaves. This soon developed into an elegant bouquet of flowers and became an almost universal feature of ceilings until the mid seventeenth century *(fig. 15)*. There is a ceiling with such a design in an upper chamber of **The Manor House, Somerton**, in the same room as a mid-sixteenth century overmantel. If the overmantel and ceiling are coeval, this is an extremely early use of floral spray decoration.

OPEN PATTERNS

In Devon and Cornwall there are three influential manor houses, **Trerice, Buckland Abbey** and **Collacombe Barton**, all with similar ceilings dated *c.*1575. These have larger-scale designs than the previous examples and may well have influenced later ceilings such as those in **Poundisford Lodge, Pitminster** *(fig. 60)*, one of which is in association with a dated overmantel of 1590. Both upper chambers here have segmental-shaped barrels, their end-wall lunettes sparingly decorated with interlocking squares, the ceilings having open patterns of thin ribs, larger in scale than those previously considered. Poundisford Lodge and Poundisford Park nearby were built *c.*1550 by two brothers very much in competition with one another. The houses are similar in style but the Lodge, although started first, has the later plasterwork.

One of the finest of the large-scale open flowing designs is the Hall ceiling at **Nutcombe Manor, Clayhanger**, on the Devon side of the border *(fig. 61)*. Here there is a huge curving pattern of thin ribs which form tulip shapes, a scheme taken direct from Walter Gedde's **Booke of Sundry Draughts** *(fig. 62)*. The tulip shapes may be fortuitous, but it is interesting to note that the passion for tulip growing in Holland was to some extent echoed in England in Jacobean times.

In houses with small rooms where the ceilings are divided into panels by downstanding beams, patterns are necessarily small-scale. At **Plud Farm, Stringston**, the Parlour ceiling

15. Floral Sprays of the early seventeenth century
a & b: *West Catford, Huish Champflower*
c: *The Gables, Stoke-sub-Hamdon*
d & e: *Montacute House*
f: *Nettlecombe Court*

is divided in this manner into four panels, each with a different pattern, one of which is a miniature version of the 'tulip' ceiling from Gedde's book. Beams in such cases are usually covered in moulded plaster with a running relief pattern on the flat underside.

In the north-east of the county, in the Frome area, ceiling designs differ from those in the south and west in often having a central pattern of radiating ribs, forming petal shapes, leaving the rest of the ceiling plain - unlike the all-over network of ribs seen elsewhere. At **Glebe House, Great Elm**, there are two such patterns where single ribs are combined with unusual flat strips and hand-modelled floral sprays *(fig. 66)*. There are two notable exceptions to the centralised designs of the area: the splendid barrel ceiling in **Beckington Abbey, Beckington**, covered all over with strapwork, described below, and a very fine ceiling in the small **Manor Farmhouse, Laverton, Lullington** *(fig. 68)*. The latter has a densely-packed thin-rib design based on quatrefoils with many large, hand-modelled floral sprays and a two-tailed mermaid. These features are more often seen in Devon than in Somerset.

SPIRALS

There is a very unusual ceiling at **Weston Farm, Wambrook**, near Chard, where the three-sided barrel has a design completely different from anything yet seen. It consists of spirals of plant forms with acorns and berries swirling away from a central circle, covering the whole of the flat part of the ceiling *(fig. 16)* and terminating at the ends of the room in what are no doubt intended to be classical vases. Here is a departure indeed. The design

16. **Weston Farm, Wambrook**
Chamber, c.1620

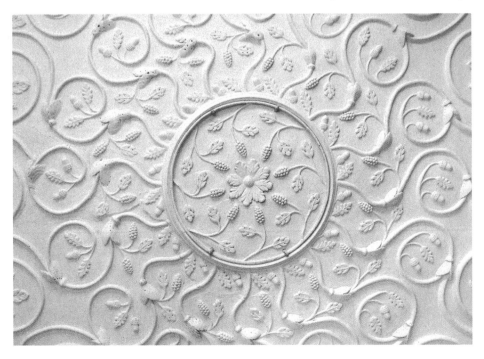

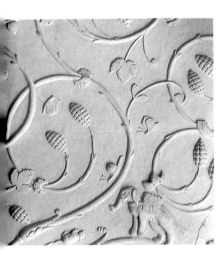

17. **Rashleigh Barton, Wembworthy, Devon**

can be linked in its overall concept with the famous early seventeenth-century ceiling in the **Butterwalk, Dartmouth**, Devon, the 'Tree of Jesse' where the spiral stems spring from the recumbent Jesse to support his many descendants and terminate at the apex with the Virgin and Child. But in Weston Farm no such ambitious scheme of figure modelling is attempted, the result a bower for a marriage chamber rather than a bible lesson. This ceiling was probably decorated at the same time as the Parlour ceiling downstairs *c.1620*. A more sophisticated ceiling at **Rashleigh Barton, Wembworthy**, Devon *(fig.17)*, has a comparable overall pattern of spirals and strawberries but here decorated with innumerable naturalistic creatures, a mouse, snails, butterflies and even an elephant, all typical of the Barnstaple 'school' of plasterers of the early seventeenth century and quite different from the stylised animals of the Parlour ceiling in Weston Farm, described below.

DOUBLE AND ENRICHED RIB CEILINGS *c.1600- c.1650*

These ceilings have much the same sort of widely-spaced patterns as already seen on the later thin-rib ceilings, but the ribs are either double - two thin ribs set closely side by side - or with ribs set more widely apart like railway lines with the space in between 'enriched' with running patterns of fruit and flowers. Double ribs are generally a little earlier in date than enriched ribs but there is a good deal of overlap between the two.

The Hall at **Nettlecombe Court** *(fig. 18 & 72)*, built 1599, has one of the finest enriched ceilings in the county with knob-like pendants and ornate floral sprays, very frilly and Jacobean. Some of the ribs are left plain and some are decorated with enrichments. The ceiling is thought to date from the early years of the seventeenth century when John Trevelyan was remodelling his Hall (the frieze with grotesque dolphins is identical with one in the Hall at **Montacute House**, *c.*1600). If this date is correct it is early for an enriched rib design. Other notable enriched rib ceilings are in the upstairs chambers at **No. 18 Fore Street, Taunton** *(fig. 51)*, with pendant and shield motifs, and in the east of the county at **Manor Cottage, Laverton, Lullington** *(fig. 67)*, a segmental barrel with an over large and ugly cage pendant its only other decoration. The lunettes in this room are decorated with large stiff thistle plants and a coat of arms of Farewell impaling Warde. Thomas Farewell married Anne Warde 1594, plasterwork perhaps by their son Thomas *c.*1630.[13] Thistles are symbolic of marital fidelity, hence the use in the best bedroom.

In three buildings in south Somerset there is some remarkable plasterwork of unusually inventive design. The Court Room, **Court House, Chard** *(fig. 63)*, is a large, airy chamber with huge windows. The wide segmental barrel ceiling has double ribs, rather wider than usual, in stellar patterns with flowers, sun, moon, stars and strange mythological beasts, all modelled in low relief and most imaginatively done. The style of the plasterer can be recognised in two other local houses - **Whitestaunton Manor**, which has a fantastic animal frieze[14] and **Weston Farm, Wambrook** *(fig. 64)*, where the low Parlour ceiling is in four panels, in each a different double-rib pattern. The Weston Farm ceiling is peopled with the most bizarre assortment of animals including a realistic lobster and human-headed beasts, combined with large leaf sprays *(fig. 124)*. The animals are similar to those in the Court Room, Chard, but at Weston Farm even more fanciful. Some of the beasts are common to both and to the Whitestaunton frieze: a crested serpent, a winged rabbit and, hidden away - a rather likeable touch - a dog with floppy ears. Similar strange animals, rather more refined in treatment and on a slightly smaller scale, occur on the Parlour ceiling at **Wigborough Manor, South Petherton** *(fig. 50)*, where the modelling in the frieze and overmantel in this room is similar to that of much of the Chard plasterwork. Wigborough and Weston Farm were connected by marriage[15] and it seems likely that the plasterwork was executed in all four houses in the 1620s or 1630s.

18. **Nettlecombe Court**
The Hall

Another ornate ceiling with many animals can be seen in the State Dining Room at **Hinton House, Hinton St George** *(fig.65)*. Although Hinton is not far from the other examples, this very accomplished ceiling derives its decoration from a group of houses in the Exeter area and is not related to the Chard designs.

STRAPWORK CEILINGS *c.1640*

In some 'prodigy' houses in England, for example Audley End or Blickling Hall, there are some fine ceilings entirely covered with branching designs in flat strapwork, but in Somerset only one has been found, the large and well-known barrel ceiling at **Beckington Abbey** *(fig. 69)*, where there is a stunning display of Caroline plasterwork. The barrel is studded with fleurs-de-lis and rosettes and the two long sides of the ceiling are cantilevered out over a wide coved cornice, itself covered with strapwork.

PENDANTS

Pendants are a conspicuous feature of the more elaborate ceilings, the earliest discovered being those at **Mapperton**, Dorset, and **Poundisford Park, Pitminster**, *c.*1550-70 *(fig. 73)*. The pendant gives dramatic emphasis to the design, the largest always in the centre of the room from which was hung a lamp or candelabrum. Early pendants are usually plain but later examples are more elaborate and have leaf and flower decorations to match in style the enriched ribs of the Jacobean period (e.g. the pendants in the Hall at **Nettlecombe Court**) *(fig. 72)*. Late Elizabethan and Jacobean pendants were sometimes made hollow - generally referred to as 'cage' pendants - with three or more curved ribs, richly decorated with creeping plants and faces around an empty centre (**Manor Cottage, Laverton**). The Elizabethan liking for cage pendants is echoed in their delight in hollowing out oak finials on staircase newels, the fashion even more impressively expressed in the stone roof- finials of the summer houses and gazebos at **Montacute House**.

By far the largest and most spectacular pendant in the area is the huge isolated example hanging above the staircase at **Chelvey Court, Chelvey**, Avon, of *c.*1665 *(fig. 19)*. This splendid decoration hangs down a full four feet and is in three stages like an inverted wedding cake, decorated with leaves and floral swags and with little sub-pendants hanging from its upper stage.

There is another staircase pendant, not so large, in **Barrow Court, Barrow Gurney**, Avon, centred on an elaborate and unique ceiling design based on medieval window tracery patterns *(fig. 74)*. Its associated giant grotesque frieze is also unique. The date is thought to be seventeenth century; (compare the plaster barrel ceiling in the nave of St John's church, **Axbridge**; a geometric network of Gothic tracery with three large pendants, one dated 1636, clearly an example of seventeenth-century romantic nostalgia which the Barrow Court staircase plasterwork may also be).

CLASSICAL *c.1640-1700*

The date range of this section overlaps with the last, but the ceilings are totally different in form, being based on the classical style introduced from Italy by Inigo Jones. Ceilings are either flat or divided by heavy plastered beams into large panels. Almost all contain a huge classical wreath or garland of fruit and flowers as the centre-piece, have wide decorated bands filling the surrounding spaces and are bordered with a properly moulded classical cornice. The parlours in even quite small houses were furnished at least with a wreath and

19. **Chelvey Court, Clevedon**
Pendant above staircase, c.1665

in the centre perhaps a family motto, an allegorical figure or even a biblical scene.

At first, the decorations in local examples were flavoured with the remains of the Jacobean style, with residual strapwork and occasional references to the grotesque, but this backward looking was soon abandoned and in the larger houses the more whole-hearted classical style was adopted, complete with rich acanthus scrolls, heavily decorated cornices and all the pompous trimmings of Italianate classicism. Ornament had become more restricted in subject matter, although carried out with such expertise and exuberance that ceilings dominate the later Stuart rooms even more than they did the Elizabethan ones.

The earliest of the classical ceilings in Somerset is in the Hall at **Gaulden Manor, Tolland**, *c.*1640 *(fig 24 & 75)*. Here the magnificent flat ceiling contains two ovals flanking a large central, circular wreath (which, untypically for the period, still sports a central pendant) with fragmentary strapwork-like scrolls around the edges of all three panels, an excellent example of the transitional style. In the centre of the ovals are stiffly-modelled biblical figures - in one the Last Trump, a winged angel blowing his trumpet above a recumbent skeleton *(fig. 20)*, in the other a benign-looking King David playing his harp *(fig 13)*. Both figures have appropriate

20. **Gaulden Manor, Tolland**
Hall, c.1640, wreath detail
'The Last Trump'

Latin inscriptions on banners. In a small adjoining room plastered beams form four panels with coved cornices and geometrical patterns containing small wreaths, identical to those in a small room in **Nettlecombe Court** *(fig. 77)*. At Nettlecombe another chamber has an oval wreath ceiling surrounded by broad bands of fruit and flowers and in the centre the Trevelyan family crest, a horse emerging from the waves. The two houses are quite near each other and the two families were later connected by marriage; surely the same plasterer worked in both.

The small merchant's house known as **Coal Harbour Farm, Ham, Creech St Michael**, is remarkable for the unexpected grandeur of its low Parlour ceiling *(fig. 11)*. There is a large oval wreath with pretty fruit and flower meanders and the central oval contains, within the usual scrolly band, a scene in low relief showing Abraham in the act of sacrificing Isaac with the angel telling him to desist. Evidently there was not enough room here for the ram caught by his horns in the thicket. This scene (with or without the ram) was extremely popular during the first half of the seventeenth century, more often in overmantels than on ceilings. A similar wreath can be seen in the Parlour wing at **Bournes, Wiveliscombe** *(fig. 76)*. Here the central oval contains Venus and Cupid with an inscribed banner in the style of the Gaulden Manor ceiling.

Such ceilings with ovals can occur in quite small houses where the rooms are low and the dominant plasterwork is only just above the heads of the occupants. By contrast, the really magnificent ceilings in **Forde Abbey**, Dorset, *c.*1655, are in huge, lofty rooms and are among the finest examples of the early classical style of plasterwork in the country *(fig. 80)*. Here the designs are clearly new to the craftsmen who treat the various elements with many backward glances to earlier styles - small grotesque figures and strapwork cartouches appearing among the more orthodox acanthus and guilloche patterns of classical Rome.

The fully-developed classical style of the 1680s, altogether more correct, can be seen at its best in **Halswell House, Goathurst**, *c.*1689. A disastrous fire in 1923 destroted part of the interior and much of the plasterwork we see today, in spite of its totally authentic appearance, is a restoration *(fig. 79)*. The great stair hall and the north-east state chamber were reinstated to their former glory with heavy wreaths, deeply undercut floral and foliated panels and classical cornices. The craftsmanship of these sumptuous ceilings is of the

21. Dunster Castle
Staircase detail, c.1680

highest quality. But perhaps the most splendid of all the classical ceilings are in **Dunster Castle**, executed a little earlier in 1681 - the aristocrat of Somerset plasterwork *(fig. 21, 23 & 78)*. Here the work is on a grander scale and is also impeccably correct, although on a close look at the staircase ceiling the acanthus scrolls are seen to entwine small figures of huntsmen, hounds and stags, an engaging conceit repeated in the magnificent carved scrollwork of the staircase balustrade.

This grand style is copied locally at **Steyning Manor, Stogursey**, where the same large-scale stiff cornice of leaves in the Dining Room at Dunster Castle is repeated in the smaller

Hall of the manor, combined with fruits and seedpods in high relief on the beams and with palm-leaf fronds and a particularly robust overmantel *(fig. 111)*, all rather overpowering in such small surroundings.

LATE CLASSICAL DESIGNS

Towards 1700 the ponderously ornate designs of the early classical style gradually gave way to altogether lighter and less overwhelming schemes of decoration. At **Farm Estate, Fiddington**, more refined and naturalistic motifs herald the last years of the century *(fig. 81 & 82)*. In the Parlour is a beautiful circular ceiling wreath made up of chains of seedpods, fruits and leaves, the corner panels having rather bucolic putti (as has Steyning Manor) surrounded by acanthus leaves. These cherubs have none of the idealised physique of classical putti, but have more the appearance of real infants modelled by a local plasterer without first-hand knowledge of his Italian prototype. Another infant occurs on the ceiling of a small ground-floor room in **Nettlecombe Court**, *c.*1700 where a similarly freely-modelled floral wreath, naturalistically done and quite different from the tight formality of the early wreaths, surround the central little boy embowered in palm leaves *(fig. 22 & 83)*. Leafy wreaths of the same naturalistic sort appear between the beams of the Parlour in **Washers, Fitzhead**.

22. **Nettlecombe Court**
Detail of naturalistic modelling, c.1700

These simpler, naturalistic designs conclude the sequence of ceilings which progresses from the stiff patterns of the early Tudors, through the thin-rib, all-over patterns of the Elizabethans and the frilly enriched Jacobean designs to the heavy formality of the true classical school that characterises the work executed after the Civil War.

23. **Dunster Castle**
Detail of staircase ceiling,
Hunting scene.

9 Sebastiano Serlio, *The Five Books of Architecture.*

10 H.A.Wyndham, *A Family History, 1410-1688; the Wyndhams of Norfolk and Somerset*, 97.

11 eg. Henry VII's Chapel, Westminster, 1500-1512; see fig. 57

12 A.W. Vivian-Neal, 'Tudor and Stuart Plasterwork in West Somerset', *Proc. Som. Arch. Soc.* xcvi (1951), 144-5.

13 Information from Mr. Michael McGarvie.

14 See p.26

15 *Visitations of Somerset, 1623*, ed. Colby, 10.

24. **Gaulden Manor, Tolland**
Hall, c.1640;
a rich transitional design

CHAPTER 3

FRIEZES

*Further illustrations
are on pages 61 to 63*

IN THE HALLS of the larger medieval houses, open to the high timbers of the roof, the junction between roof and wall was usually closed with short, vertical timbers called 'ashlaring' which carried a horizontal strip of carved decoration along the long sides of the room. This medieval carving at the top of the wall paved the way for the acceptance of classical friezes in the flat-ceiled halls and chambers of the sixteenth century, for at least the idea of a high-level strip of decoration came as no novelty even if the forms and patterns of the new work were entirely of the Renaissance, owing little to medieval traditions.

The frieze, high up and relatively difficult to see in any detail, was a less dominant decorative feature than either ceiling or overmantel and consequently provided an opportunity for the introduction of imaginative designs that could be taken less seriously than those decorating the more prominent elements. The ornate formality of the highly

*25. **Mapperton, Dorset***
Great Chamber frieze, c.1550

accomplished, dense-packed early Tudor designs, executed for the Court by Italian craftsmen, had by the mid sixteenth century been adopted in the provinces. The Great Chamber frieze in **Mapperton House**, Dorset, *c.*1550, is typical of its date, with a very Tudor feature, small wreathed medallions containing renaissance heads *(fig. 25)*. Here the medallions are supported by human half-figures whose legs trail off into curled-up, foliated mermaid tails. The 'Antike' friezes at **Poundisford Park, Pitminster**, *c.*1570, are very similar in general feeling and execution but without the medallions and with a greater emphasis on fierce monster heads growing out of the leafy scrollwork *(fig. 84 & 85)*.

The terms Antike or Antic implied both the playful nature of the designs and their ancient origins. The intricate style was ideally suited to the narrow plaster friezes of the time. By the end of the sixteenth century the style had entered a phase where total freedom of invention was acceptable, although still strictly within the elegant discipline of flowing renaissance lines. Henry Peacham, writing *c.*1600, described the Antike style of his day as *"an unnaturall or unorderly composition for delight sake, of men, beasts, birds, fishes, flowers etc and without (as wee say) Rime or reason, for the greater variety you shew in your invention, the more you please ... naked boys riding ... uppon Goates, eagles, Dolphins, etc ... Satyres, Tritons, apes, Cornucopias ... cherries and any kind of wild trail or vine after your owne invention ... so that herein you cannot be too fantastical."* [16]

This splendid if rather high-flown passage describes the style rather well, although all the fantastic elements are unlikely to be found together in any one piece. Heavily foliated spirals and scrollwork, usually with monsters or putti, was referred to as 'Forest Work', but Antike, Forest Work, Savage Work and Grotesque seem to have been more or less interchangeable terms for the style in Elizabethan and Jacobean times.

NARROW FRIEZES

There are many examples of the truly grotesque in the narrow friezes, 5" to 9" deep, which were almost universally used until the end of the sixteenth century, and in small houses until about forty years later. The Gallery frieze in **Poundisford Park** is a good example of the style. A similar design can also be seen in **Holcombe Court, Holcombe Rogus**, Devon, where some nineteenth-century plaster casts used as moulds for repair work survive. Although made of plaster and not carved in wood, these casts give a very good idea of what the original moulds looked like and it is interesting to compare the moulds with the finished work. Instances where the same mould has been used in different houses are not uncommon. An example of shared moulds (*c*.1600) can be seen in the narrow Hall friezes of **Montacute House** and **Nettlecombe Court**, the design in this instance being a rather stiff pattern of leaves and dolphins without the bravura of earlier work. Where houses are in the same neighbourhood this re-use of moulds is hardly surprising, each family or firm of plasterers carrying out many commissions in its own area. More to be wondered at is the great variety of designs that speaks for the creativity and originality of the craftsmen.

There is one instance of shared moulds which deserves special mention, that of the frieze or wall decoration in the Great Chamber of **Haddon Hall**, far away in Derbyshire. Here the plasterer created a frieze about 4'0" deep, using no less than five strips of decoration, one above the other, each strip being a frieze design in its own right. It is of great interest to find that the moulds used are those found in both **Poundisford Park** and **Holcombe Court**, an amazing example of the way in which sixteenth-century craftsmen moved around the country.[17] Of course it is impossible to tell whether Poundisford Park and Holcombe Court were using frieze moulds from Derbyshire or vice versa, but it is tempting to imagine the skilled West-Country plasterers being sent for to decorate a house, however far away. The Haddon Hall plasterwork is also of interest as an example of an attempt to provide a deep space with decoration before large-scale designs had been worked out, the plasterer here merely piling one known pattern upon another until the space was filled.

For sheer exuberance and imagination the Elizabethan frieze in the Peacock Chamber in **Orchard Wyndham, Williton** *(fig. 26 & 87)*, a design of almost Shakesperian richness of concept, must be pre-eminent. Here the plasterer has invented a series of panels which repeat around the room divided by vertical balusters and freely designed vase or leaf motifs. Each panel contains a separate design of astonishing originality. There is a mermaid with a leafy tail supported by curiously truncated birds; there are vases, naive putti riding on animals and gnomes with tall noddy-hats; there are dolphins and cherubs, flowers and seaweed-like foliage; and the peacocks, which give their name to the chamber, have fine crests and again are truncated so that their tails disappear. All this is executed in a stiff, naive style of great charm and vitality. The motifs are nearly all derived from classical designs, but it is evident that although the craftsman had seen them, either in books or in other houses, he preferred to re-invent them in his own individual way and created in the process one of the most striking pieces of relief design in the county.

26. Orchard Wyndham, Williton
Peacock frieze, late sixtenth century

An example of the antike style being used in later work, perhaps using an older mould, is represented in the frieze in **Beckington Abbey** Great Chamber, installed *c*.1640 *(fig. 88)*. This fine frieze incorporates fierce bearded monster heads with shields supported by winged creatures, all in a scrolly trail of fruit and flowers. Only slightly less grotesque is the frieze in the small house, **Yea Cottage, Cushuish, Cothelstone** *(fig. 92)*, which sports a monkey, a bunch of grapes and a dragon's head which together form a repeat pattern based on spiralling meanders of leaves and tendrils. The same pattern occurs on an upstairs chimney-piece in the house, but installed upside-down so that the monkey stands on his head. The chimney-piece is dated 1674 so presumably the plasterer who decorated it took a cast from the earlier frieze downstairs and inverted it by mistake.

Other grotesque designs are found in Somerset farmhouses where a stiff simplicity of execution shows clearly the hand of the simple country plasterer. A design incorporating a vase with supporting cockatrices survives in a damaged condition above the inserted ceiling of a bedroom in **West Catford, Huish Champflower** *(fig. 27)*. Associated with this frieze are rigid flowers standing up in a row, showing all the unselfconscious directness of expression of the vernacular craftsman *(fig. 15)*.

27. West Catford Huish Champflower
A 'Cockatrice' frieze, early seventeenth century

Wherever designs have been copied and re-copied, little by little the design deteriorates often to a point where the original is scarcely recognisable, as in Dark Age barbarian copies of Roman coins, where a Roman chariot and horses in the original is reduced in the copy to one wheel and some detached horses' hooves. An example of the same thing in plaster can be seen in the frieze-like decoration of the ceiling beams at **Priors Farm, Stringston** *(fig. 46 & 89)*, where upstanding creatures which may originally have been dolphins oppose one another with, between their tails, what evidently started life as a fluted vase, here virtually dismembered so that little but the flutes remain. These and other unsophisticated examples have some basis of classical formality about them, but in the simplest decorative scheme so far seen, in **Cathanger Farm, Stogursey**, two motifs, in this case a bird alternating with a flower, are merely repeated at widely-spaced intervals around the room.

FLAT FRETS

A far cry from such simple schemes are the highly developed designs called 'flat frets'. Using the basic patterns of strapwork but without the interweaving three-dimensional features of the style, formal repetitive abstract patterns are raised above a flat background like applique fretwork or cut-out card. Such patterns are found on friezes and on fireplaces (**Court House, East Quantoxhead**). Perhaps the best known frieze in this style is in the Parlour of **Montacute House** where the pattern is combined with a series of shields showing the Phelips arms alternating with panels containing small animals *(fig. 99)*.

Development of the flat fret technique applied to a running meander rather than to a strapwork pattern resulted in a very simple repeat such as in the tulip frieze of the **Gate House, Combe Florey** *(fig. 90)* (associated with an overmantel dated 1593) or in the anthemion frieze in the White Chamber, **Poundisford Lodge, Pitminster**, *c*.1590. In these designs the dominant motif, tulip or anthemion, is simplified and flattened and repeats, alternately right way up and upside-down, with plain flat scrolls between to link the motifs together. These simple but powerful patterns repeat all round the room without variety or elaboration, a curiously restrained design not the least allied to the grotesque or antike.

THIN-STEMMED SPIRALS

Another marked departure from the grotesque style of the sixteenth century is what may be called the 'Thin-stemmed Spiral'. The style came into fashion *c*.1615 and features stylised plant forms with extravagantly thin stems arranged in regular spirals, the sparse foliage and flowers showing a great deal of plain background. Designs in this style are found decorating friezes and the end walls of barrel-ceiled chambers (for example, the frieze at **The Croft, Washford, Old Cleeve** *(fig. 93)*, and the chamber walls of **Little Court, West Bagborough**, and of **Marshwood Farm, Carhampton**). The well preserved frieze in The Croft is an admirable example of the style at its most straightforward. There is a very decorative but more elementary version of this type of frieze pattern which comprises a simple meander with bunches of grapes, the one sinuous stem going over and under regularly-spaced flowers so stylised that they look more like bicycle wheels than flowers. This robust design was evidently popular since it occurs in three houses: **The Gables, Stoke sub Hamdon** *(fig. 95)*; **Wyndhams, Marston Magna**, not far away and, a good deal farther off, in **Forsters, Shapwick**. The design is probably of the early to mid seventeenth century, but in the case of Forsters associated plasterwork is dated 1712, so if that date also applies to the frieze the craftsmen were using a very old mould.

DEEP FRIEZES

After *c*.1600 friezes in the big rooms of the larger houses were laid out on a more lavish scale which demanded an entirely new approach to frieze design. **Montacute House** has friezes over 3'0" deep, designed to fit the various rooms as carefully worked out overall decorative schemes *(fig. 97)*. The friezes here are divided by decorated vertical strips into rectangular panels each containing a design. In the Crimson Chamber the designs are of floral sprays and in the Library of strapwork cartouches, shields and swags of fruit.

At **Wigborough Manor, South Petherton**, there is an unusual flat-fret and strapwork frieze, 2'6" deep, designed on a large scale with very simple details *(fig. 98)*. The design contains panels showing scenes that are as naively executed as the overmantel in the same room. There is a hunting scene which may be a Death of Actaeon and, equally enigmatic, on another plaque a man and a woman in Jacobean dress stand either side of a narrow structure that may be a well. A deep strapwork frieze such as this is unique in the writers' experience in Somerset.

28. **Whitestaunton Manor**
Great Chamber, c.1630;
the most startlingly original
frieze in Somerset

Mention has already been made of the extraordinary frieze in the Great Chamber of **Whitestaunton Manor** *(fig. 28)*. This unique example, executed *c*.1630, has an amazing wealth of imaginatively designed creatures modelled in low relief, each one more weird than the last and all different. Although the frieze is not particularly deep, approximately 22", the scale is large and the style not at all like that of the narrower friezes considered earlier in the chapter. Nor does the design appear to owe anything whatever to French, Flemish or Italian sources. There is a human-headed lion, a shoal of leaping fish, a splendid mermaid with a hooked nose and flowing hair, a plumed serpent with a jaunty expression, a lion-headed beast with two bodies, an ostrich holding a horseshoe in its beak[18] and many more besides including the dog's head which forms, as it does in the **Court House, Chard** *(fig. 91)*, the terminal of one of the leafy branches which weld the whole frieze together with a more or less continuous foliated trail. At one end of the room is a coat of arms which helps to date the frieze, showing Brett impaling White; the marriage of Sir Robert Brett and Mary White, took place *c.1630.*[19]

TRANSITIONAL

A good deal of work executed in the 1640s is transitional between the fully-developed classical style and the Jacobean which preceded it and in such cases friezes, in combination with heavily-wreathed ceilings, are not uncommon. The Hall and Inner Parlour in **Gaulden Manor, Tolland**, have deep friezes in the swirling floral and foliated fashion of the mid seventeenth century *(fig. 29)*. Such designs, opulent in conception and accomplished in execution, have flowers moulded as though seen from the side, either pendant like fuschias or upstanding. In the Gaulden Manor frieze the floral pattern is punctuated by scenes symbolising the life of James Turberville, Bishop of Exeter (imprisoned in the Tower where he is thought to have died) whose great nephew, John Turberville, went to live in Gaulden in 1642 and almost certainly installed the plasterwork then or very soon afterwards.[20] John was evidently proud enough of his family connection to commemorate his great uncle in this way. The scenes depicted are in cartouches or on rather decadently asymmetrical shields around the room, some with captions in Latin.

29. **Gaulden Manor**, Tolland
Hall, c.1640

There is another quite unique transitional-style frieze in the small Dining Room at **Nettlecombe Court** *(fig. 96)* in association with an overmantel dated 1641. The frieze runs between classically-moulded downstanding beams supported on acanthus brackets and comprises a strikingly robust form of simplified large-scale key pattern with leafy terminals.

CLASSICAL

After these exuberant early designs the truly classical friezes in rooms decorated in the heavy 'Inigo Jones' style of the post Civil War period come as something of a disappointment. In general terms the frieze, as a distinct architectural element, becomes subservient to a dominating cornice and in many cases is absent altogether.

The foliated scrollwork frieze in the huge Saloon in **Forde Abbey**, Dorset, 1657, is so overpowered by the elaborate cornice and the massive ceiling as to be scarcely noticeable. The true classical idiom would demand a frieze of swags or garlanded ox-skulls, but only one of this type has been found by the writers in Somerset, the Dining Room frieze in **Dunster Castle**, *c.1681*, which comprises heavy moulded swags or garlands of fruit and flowers reminiscent of the work of Grinling Gibbons *(fig. 30)*.

30. **Dunster Castle**
*Dining Room, 1681;
a classical frieze*

By the end of the century when delicate open-work ceiling wreaths were fashionable and the heavy designs of the mid to late seventeenth century were a thing of the past, friezes were very seldom installed. The period of wonderful inventiveness was over and only a thin, beribboned trail of leaves takes the place of the masterly creations of the Elizabethan and Jacobean craftsmen.

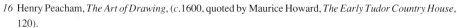

16 Henry Peacham, *The Art of Drawing,* (*c.*1600, quoted by Maurice Howard, *The Early Tudor Country House*, 120).

17 A.W. Vivian-Neal, 'Tudor and Stuart Plasterwork in West Somerset', *Proc. Som. Arch. Soc.* xcvi. The Haddon connection with the West Country may have been through the marriage of Elizabeth Manners to Sir William Courtenay of Powderham: Burke, *Peerage* (1949), p.1749.

18 An ostrich holding a horseshoe is the crest of the Digby family.

19 *Proc. Som. Arch. Soc.* xxviii (1882), 86.

20 Ibid. cxvi (1972), 113-14.

31. **Wigborough Manor**
South Petherton
c.1630

CHAPTER *4*

OVERMANTELS *and* WALL DECORATIONS

*Further illustrations
are on pages 64 to 66*

THE IMPORTANCE OF THE FIREPLACE in our damp, dark, northern climate hardly needs restating. The hearth was not only a source of life-enhancing heat and in earlier houses the means of cooking meat, but was until the eighteenth century, even in the grandest houses, a principal source of light. As the centre or focus of the house, its importance was transferred from the medieval open hearth blazing in the centre of the Hall, to the fireplace and chimney-piece when those were introduced in the sixteenth century. Castles and stone-built houses of importance, usually ecclesiastical, had chimneys long before then, but the generality of houses great and small had no such convenience until *c.*1500-50.

Late-medieval overmantels can be seen carved in wood or stone in a few surviving great houses and monasteries. An outstanding Somerset example is the overmantel in the Abbot's Lodgings in Muchelney Abbey where, above the rectangular fireplace opening, four stone-carved quatrefoils beneath a stiff-leaved vine trail are flanked by tall gothic pilasters supporting heraldic lions, all in the late Perpendicular style of *c.*1500.

Undoubtedly the grandest and most ornate early renaissance chimney-pieces are in France and Italy. Perhaps Francis I's huge carved and gilded fireplaces in the chateau at Blois are the most magnificent; overpowering in size, glittering with gold leaf, these great splurges of dynastic pride take the breath away as much today as they were intended to do in the early years of the sixteenth century when they were installed. In England nothing so opulent survives, although no doubt Henry VIII's Nonsuch, built in the 1520s to compete with Francis's palaces, would have had similar fireplaces, since he employed some of the same Italian workmen as did Francis.

As the focus of the house, the chimney-piece was the natural place for a display of decoration, but decoration with a purpose; that of demonstrating to the world the wealth, breeding, education and importance of the owners. Here they proudly displayed their coats of arms, many newly acquired under the Tudors, with supporting figures or flanking caryatids and carved mottoes, all in surrounds of scrollwork or strapwork, the latest fashion in late Elizabethan and Jacobean times.

Not only the Hall was provided with a fireplace. Upper chambers, too, had fireplaces with overmantels, here sometimes displaying a biblical, allegorical or classical scene as the centrepiece of the design, the family coat of arms more often being given pride of place downstairs in the Hall where visitors could see it. The sheer quantity and variety of overmantels in this part of England means that only a few examples can be given to illustrate the different types of design.

The earliest plaster overmantels found in Somerset occur in the upper chambers of two houses in the Glastonbury area: **Higher Southtown Farm, West Pennard** *(fig. 32)*, and the **Manor House, Somerton**.

The first, although cracked and distorted by the sloping ceiling, is a dramatic survival in a small house of great quality. It comprises a square of densely-patterned decorative batons set lozenge-wise round a floral fleur-de-lis with smaller fleurs-de-lis round the outside. The

32. **Higher Southtown Farm
West Pennard**
*Chamber,
mid-sixteenth century*

29

plasterwork is undated, but decorative batons were popular motifs in Tudor times and the intricate small-scale nature of the modelling is typical of the Italianate taste of the early to mid sixteenth century.

A much grander edition of the design, also undated, is in the Wing Chamber at **Mapperton**, Dorset *(fig. 33)*. Here a lozenge of the same decorated batons contains a coat of arms of the Morgans while round the outside, instead of fleurs-de-lis, are four roundels containing renaissance heads cast from the same moulds as used for the Great Chamber frieze in the same house. The overmantel is completed by serpentine vine trails and elaborately decorated flanking balusters or columnettes. There is little doubt that the same mould was used in both houses for the batons, but no connection between West Pennard and the Morgans of Mapperton has yet been found.

33. **Mapperton**, **Dorset**
Overmantel,
mid sixteenth century

Similar in style to those two overmantels is the recently painted and well preserved overmantel in the **Manor House, Somerton** *(fig. 35)*. Here the elegant design incorporates the Dodington arms in a plainly moulded lozenge with fleurs-de-lis, on a panel supported by two decorated columnettes. The columnettes are identical to those of the Mapperton overmantel and are surely from the same mould.

All three overmantels are contemporary and may be dated to the 1550s. By the 1590s the aesthetic had entirely changed. Designs by then had the fashionable Flemish flavour, much bolder in scale and displaying a wealth of strapwork and figures, either in high relief or modelled in the round. Of these the finest and most elaborate is in the principal upper chamber known as the Tudor Room in the **Gatehouse, Combe Florey**, dated 1593 *(fig. 34)*. Half-figures or terms, male and female, stand two on each side of a central panel containing a strapwork cartouche with a whole achievement of arms of the Frauncis family - shield,

34. **Gatehouse**, **Combe Florey**
Tudor Room, 1593

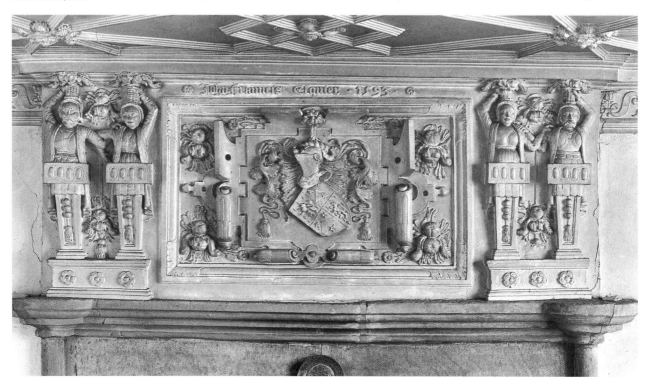

helm, crest and elaborate mantle, all beautifully executed and with an inscription and date above. This is clearly the work of a master craftsman, almost certainly Robert Eaton, a Somerset man (See Chapter 5).

CARYATIDS AND TERMS

Flanking figures (as distinct from heraldic supporters on either side of a coat of arms) standing on each side of an overmantel, more often one at a time than in pairs as at Combe Florey, became very popular in the last part of the sixteenth and the first half of the seventeenth centuries. Such figures usually represent a virtue or other concept, such as Hope, Faith, Peace or Justice each with his, or more often her, distinguishing symbol (See Chapter 1). Male figures are usually bearded or given moustaches; female ones have long dresses, in some cases with skirts split to show one elegant leg. Such figures are for convenience referred to as caryatids, although a caryatid is strictly speaking always female and is in the form of a column supporting an entablature on her head. In contrast, these plasterwork figures balance baskets of fruit on their heads, often without any crowning entablature.

35. **Manor House, Somerton**
Chamber; detail of colonette

The origins of the idea of incorporating flanking figures on either side of the overmantel came from France where mid sixteenth century examples can be seen in the chateaux of the Loire, for example the overmantel in Diane de Poitiers' chamber in Chenonceaux carved by Jean Goujon c.1550. The large stone figures in Longleat, carved by the Frenchman Alain Maynard in 1563, may well have been the inspiration for this fashion in Somerset, introduced some thirty years later perhaps by William Arnold, whose father worked at Longleat as a joiner. William himself, a mason, is known to have worked at Montacute House and Dunster Castle c.1600.[21] Terms or half-figures, whose lower halves are formed of square tapering columns or some other more or less architectural feature, are sometimes used as flanking figures, as in the Combe Florey overmantel, instead of full-length caryatids. The unnatural idea of a term is taken from classical Rome, and terms are normally only used in the more elaborate and sophisticated designs. Terms, more simply designed, can be see at **Dunster Castle**, dated 1620, and a more primitive example in the Parlour of **Wigborough Manor, South Petherton** *(fig. 31 & 100)*.

COATS OF ARMS

Coats of arms form an almost universal element in the decoration of the larger houses. The more opulently designed overmantels have the entire achievement of arms as in Combe Florey, others only the shield. Coats of arms were important to the sixteenth- and seventeenth-century house owner. They established his family history and, if he had made an advantageous marriage, that of his wife. They also ensured that everyone knew that he was a gentleman. If the householder was anxious to commemorate a particularly illustrious or well connected ancestor or relative, his arms would also be incorporated in the design. A striking example of this is in the Hall overmantel in **Gaulden Manor, Tolland**, which has no less than four coats of arms - at the top the owner's (Turberville), at the foot Turbervlle impaling Willoughby (John Turberville married Bridget Willoughby in 1639)[22], and on either side Turberville impaling Carew and Norris, showing how well connected the Turbervilles were. Upstairs in the Hall Chamber of the same house is a full achievement of arms commemorating John's marriage to Bridget, with beautifully executed supporters in the form of fish-tailed bears held in strapwork collars to the central cartouche *(fig. 101)*.

These arms, too, can safely be dated to *c*.1640, but here the achievement lacks a crest which was crudely lopped off when the bedroom ceiling was lowered. The fireplace lintel on which this overmantel rests is decorated with very finely moulded running scrollwork. The decoration is made from the same mould as that used for a similar lintel in the transitional style fireplace at **Nettlecombe Court**. The latter is dated 1641 and both overmantels are almost certainly by the same highly accomplished hand.

A show of Royal Arms was an important affirmations of loyalty, particularly when the Tudor dynasty was new. Reference has already been made to the Royal Arms in the Great Chamber at Lytes Cary. Royal Arms are sometimes displayed over important fireplaces, as in the Hall in **Rowlands, Ashill**, where the arms of Elizabeth I form the overmantel in a decorated lozenge-frame between elongated flanking pilasters. Above is the motto (LIFE) AND DEATH ARE OF GOD. Alternatively, Royal Arms are located as wall panels at the high end of the Hall as in **Poundisford Park** where the owner would sit symbolically beneath his sovereign *(fig. 73)*. Here the display of arms is identical to that in Rowlands and the decorations in the lozenge-frames are both from the same mould.

Coats of arms other than those of royalty are occasionally displayed as wall decoration rather than in overmantels. A good late example can be seen in the Hall of **Church Close, Goathurst** *(fig. 113)*, formerly the manor house of Goathurst manor.[23] The arms show Buncombe impaling Paulet (John Buncombe married Mary Paulet in 1650)[24] in an elaborate cartouche sprouting palm leaves, all recently coloured in heraldic tints. The arms were evidently erected a good deal later than the marriage they commemorated as the whole achievement is executed in a classical style appropriate to the end of the century, comparable to that of the plasterwork in the Great Chamber at **Halswell House** nearby, *c*.1690.

SCENES IN CARTOUCHES

The fashion for incorporating a scene from the bible or from classical mythology as the centre-piece of an overmantel appears in Elizabethan and Jacobean times to have stemmed from an enthusiasm for learning and perhaps as a means of demonstrating the owner's piety and education.

Of all the plasterwork scenes, by far the most popular was Abraham sacrificing Isaac. Among many overmantels depicting the event, the one in **Marshwood Farm, Carhampton**, now in the porch and evidently positioned there from elsewhere, is perhaps the most endearing *(fig. 36)*. In the octagonal central panel of a heavy strapwork cartouche, the bearded Abraham in Jacobean clothes is shown about to draw his sword, his other hand laid affectionately on Isaac's head. Isaac is shown as a seventeenth-century teenager in knee breeches in an attitude of prayer on the sacrifical pyre of logs; a calm ram stands nearby in a 'thicket' while an angel face peers down at the scene through a swirl of stylised clouds.

Also in Marshwood Farm porch facing the Abraham and Isaac is another and most unusual overmantel. Similarly re-positioned from elsewhere, it depicts the story of Naboth's Vineyard (I Kings 21). On the right, Naboth is 'set on high' and is being stoned; on the left, the guilty Ahab is ploughing the vineyard and his son, on whom the Lord vowed to bring his evil (having let the wretched Ahab off) is shown as a babe in swaddling clothes, the whole scene being set outside the city walls with the city gate in the background; surely not a very pleasant story to have so graphically illustrated above a domestic fireplace. The

36. Marshwood Farm, Carhampton
'Abraham and Isaac'

panels and cartouches are clearly of the early seventeenth century and are executed in the robust naive style of the period. Marshwood Farm, together with **Court House, East Quantoxhead**, and **Dunster Castle** was owned by the Luttrell family. The farmhouse, which contains much other plasterwork, was built by George Luttrell (died 1629) for his son.

In contrast, the plasterwork in Court House itself, remodelled by George Luttrell, is far more sophisticated in concept. Here a remarkable number of overmantels in parlours and chambers throughout the house include bible scenes. These are all executed by the same hand and are almost certainly taken from engravings (probably Flemish) of renaissance paintings; their provenance has not been established. Unlike the Marshwood Farm example, the figures are all in biblical or classical dress and are not at all naive in concept. There is a Deposition, an Entry into Jerusalem, a Christ with the Little Children, an Agony in the Garden *(fig. 37)* and others. Each is framed like a picture which is surrounded by strapwork and most are flanked by caryatids or terms. All were executed *c.*1620. A more elaborate achievement of arms in the Hall, with George Luttrell's initials, displays later design features and is dated 1629 *(fig. 2)*. Two more robustly styled overmantels are in wing chambers, one with the Luttrell coat of arms flanked by Hope and Justice and dated 1614, the other a central oval containing a mermaid with comb and glass. She has sea-horses' legs at the front and a long serpent's tail with which she entraps her victim, presumably an allegory of retribution for sins of the flesh.

A magnificent overmantel in a bedchamber in the **Luttrell Arms Hotel, Dunster**, has a classical scene showing the Death of Actaeon in an oval frame *(fig. 38)*. Three hounds are enthusiastically attacking the recumbent Actaeon beneath three stylised trees to represent the forest. Female caryatids in split skirts flank the central strapwork cartouche (with hanging fruit, masks and putti) while above in a sort of pediment is a bearded figure in Jacobean clothes, presumably representing the lord of the manor, George Luttrell, who leans out over the cornice as though to deliver a sermon. He is flanked by obelisks and lions

Below:
37. **Court House, East Quantoxhead**
'The Agony in the Garden'
c.1620
Bottom:
38. **The Luttrell Arms Hotel, Dunster**
'The Death of Actaeon'
early seventeenth century

holding armorial shields carrying the royal leopards and fleurs-de-lis. The style of the plasterwork can be dated to *c*.1620; altogether one of the most striking designs in the county.

LARGE-SCALE SCENES

Overmantels wholly made of scenes without other decoration than flanking figures are of an entirely different sort. In the main chamber of **Binham Farm, Old Cleeve**, there is an outstanding example of the genre, unique in Somerset *(fig. 39)*. It has been described as representing the Seasons, but in fact it depicts the Triumph of Time.[26] Petrarch (1304-74) wrote the poetical work *I Trionfi* describing the various Triumphs (of Love, Chastity, Death, etc.) which were illustrated by renaissance artists. Flemish engravers such as Van de Noort published copies which were popular in the late sixteenth and early seventeenth centuries.

39. **Binham Farm**, Old Cleeve
'The Triumph of Time'
early seventeenth century

Triumphal scenes are quite rare in plasterwork. In Binham Farm Time is represented by the winged figure of an old man on crutches standing on a triumphal car, a sort of chariot, drawn by two antlered deer. (Deer are chosen to draw his car because, like Time, they are swift). Supporting figures surround the car - children, a youth and adults - while in the background are an old man with a stick and an infant in a walking frame. There is another Triumph of Time in Devon at **Dean Head, Swimbridge**, but rather smaller and with the action facing the other way, right to left *(fig. 118)*. This panel has also been misinterpreted as the Seasons.

The huge and very well known panel stretching right across the room at the high end of the Hall at **Montacute House** depicting 'The Skimmington Ride' *(fig. 1)*, although not an overmantel, is worth mentioning in this context because the striking similarity in the general treatment of both figures and background suggests very forcibly that it and the Binham Farm panel are by the same hand. Why grand and highly-educated people like the Phelipses, who built Montacute at the end of the sixteenth century, should want such a curiously crude and bucolic scene in their Hall remains a mystery.

Picture plaques used as overmantels are by no means confined to large houses. In the best bedroom in **Parsonage Farm, Over Stowey**, a farmhouse with an upper floor partly in the roof space, there is a simple and charming Adam and Eve, the top right hand corner of the plaque cut off at an angle by the slope of the bedroom ceiling *(fig. 103)*. The Serpent offers Eve the apple which she appears to be declining, while Adam seems already to have an apple, an early example, perhaps, of feminist revolt against the popularly-held belief that it was All Her Fault. Both figures hold modest fig leaves and the Garden of Eden is represented by three stiff but exuberant flowers.

INITIALS AND DATES

Overmantels which are simply a vehicle for the display of initials and dates are not uncommon. In the simpler schemes little other decoration is added, but the more opulent designs in the larger houses can have a full overmantel of strapwork and a central cartouche on which the owner shows his initials and perhaps those of his wife.

In the Oak Room at **Poundisford Lodge, Pitminster**, there is a fine strapwork overmantel *(fig. 105)* with the date 1590 and the initials W S and E S (for William Symes and his wife Elizabeth, daughter of Robert Hill).[27] The Hills built Poundisford Lodge, so William evidently came to live in his wife's house. The spirit and details of the design bear a marked similarity to the overmantels in **Montacute House**, *c.*1600, those in the Crimson and Garden chambers in particular. In Poundisford Lodge naked figures (hardly putti) perch on strapwork scrolls, as they do in Montacute, on either side of the central cartouche, a concept taken from Vredeman de Vries's pattern book.[28]

On a far simpler scale, the Chamber overmantel in the **Old Manse, Beckington**, has a rectangular frame outlined with plain mouldings containing a simple, low-relief design of a stiff, tulip-like plant, two meagre fleurs-de-lis, the initials I W and the date 1670 *(fig. 40)*.

40. **The Old Manse, Beckington**
Chamber, 1670

PRIMITIVE WORKMANSHIP

There is a fine example of primitive workmanship in the overmantel in the Parlour of **Priors Farm, Stringston**[29] *(fig. 41)*. This is the house with the grotesque frieze that has deteriorated by repeated copying into scarcely recognisable elements.[30] The overmantel is so wild in design yet so complicated in layout as to seem hardly the work of an adult but, having stood the test of time, it is evident that the technique and workmanship are good. This may well have been made by

41. **Prior's Farm, Stringston**
Parlour, 1658

someone, perhaps a plasterer's mate, who was used to preparing backgrounds and mixing plaster and who had an extensive vocabulary of motifs in his memory but no more design ability than a child. The result is what may be termed 'pastry-cook' plasterwork which has hand-moulded motifs applied to the background almost at random. Symmetry has, however, been preserved with stubby caryatids at either end standing hand on hip. A central plaque, with the initials G P I for George Prior and his wife and the date 1658, is flanked by panels with bunches of fruit, a sunflower and a plant.

ARCADES

The flowery style of the Jacobean period is well exemplified in the overmantels based on an arcade of (typically three) floral arches. There are several examples of the style, all in the same area around Taunton; by far the best preserved is in the main bedroom of **Hankridge Farm, West Monkton** *(fig. 42)*. A series of semi-circular arches containing stylised leaves, shells or peacock tails had been a favourite motif for carvings on furniture and chimney-pieces since Elizabethan times, and at Hankridge the design appears in cast plaster, made up almost entirely of flowers. Underneath the arches are strange gnome-like, bonneted creatures (mermaids?) embowered in foliage; the arches themselves are

42. Top right:
Ashe Farm, Thornfalcon
Bottom right:
Hankridge Farm, West Monkton
Left:
Detail of Hankridge Farm
Two 'Arcade' designs using the same moulds, c.1610

supported on grotesquely-distorted pillars while angels fill the spandrels above. The same moulds have been used for a similar overmantel in **Ashe Farm, Thornfalcon**, where the pillars have been cast the other way up and the guardian angels omitted *(fig. 42)*. The Hankridge overmantel was uncovered recently by the owner who noticed a plain rendered panel on the bedroom wall and, thinking there might be something behind it, attempted to chip it off. At once the render fell away, revealing the entirely undamaged plasterwork, clean and sharply defined just as it had left the plasterer's hand. All the accumulated layers of whitewash that normally blur the detail had come away with the render and left the plaster as good as new. Other examples of this style are at **King's Gatchell, Trull**, and **Kittisford Barton, Stawley**, the former with the Royal Arms of James I, which may help to date the other arcades.

TRANSITIONAL

The transitional style between Jacobean and classical, where both styles are used on the same overmantel, is well demonstrated in a wing chamber in **Nettlecombe Court, Nettlecombe**, the home of the Trevelyan family *(fig. 43)*. A fine central coat of arms in a strapwork cartouche with hanging bunches of fruit is flanked on either side not by caryatids but by early classical brackets with acanthus leaves; all this under a classically-moulded cornice with egg-and-dart enrichment. The coat of arms itself is of interest and shows Strode impaling Wyndham, the arms of Margaret (nee Wyndham, died 1643), wife of Sir Robert

43. **Nettlecombe Court**
Wing Chamber, c.1640

Strode, who came to live at Nettlecombe with her married daughter. In a downstairs overmantel is a shield showing Trevelyan impaling Strode, the initials M S and the date 1641 for Margaret's daughter Margaret Strode, first wife of George Trevelyan (died 1653).[31]

CLASSICAL

Overmantels, whether in stone, wood or plaster, having had a century and more of popularity, seem to have gone out of fashion quite suddenly at the Restoration, when the new classical interiors came in. To this general rule there is one outstanding exception, the Hall overmantel in **Steyning Manor, Stogursey** *(fig.111)*. As part of the rather overpowering plaster decoration, all in heavy classical style with acanthus leaf friezes and floral beams, the overmantel dominates the room. Large flowers, foliated spirals, two well-modelled amorini and two frowning masks surround a blank central cartouche of flowing classical shape with no hint of strapwork. This design, although undated, is probably of the 1670s or 1680s.

In contrast, old fashioned householders or plasterers continued to install out-dated designs in full-blooded strapwork until well after the Restoration. An anachronistic example of this sort can be seen in a bedroom of **Chilton Trivet Farm, Cannington**,[32] carrying the initials F I C for Francis Cridland and his wife and the date 1662 *(fig. 109)*. Here the simple large-scale strapwork of the overmantel, otherwise unadorned, would be more appropriate to the 1620s than the 1660s.

The more up-to-date fireplaces of the Restoration period were austere affairs, relying on their proportions and heavy bolection mouldings for effect, without overmantels at all. This was a period of elaborate whole-room wall panelling with painted landscapes or portraits in the panels over the fireplaces. Later, in the eighteenth century, gilt mirrors replaced over-mantels and decorative plasterwork was confined almost entirely to cornices and ceilings.

WALL DECORATIONS

Wall decorations comprise isolated motifs or plaques, designs in the lunettes or half-round end walls above the frieze of barrel-ceiled chambers, and one rare integrated scheme of plasterwork decorating the whole of a small room.

Generally, the decorations in lunettes follow in charaacter their ceiling designs. Thus in **Poundisford Lodge** and **Beckington Abbey** the decorations are respectively of interlocking single-rib squares and strapwork. Similarly, Henry VIII's arms on the end walls of the Great Chamber in **Lytes Cary** give point to the Tudor ceiling.[33]

The great lunettes in the Court Room of the **Court House, Chard**, one of the grandest upper rooms in the county, are of quite a different order *(fig. 44)*. Here the plasterer has given full rein to his imagination and decorated the two lunettes with figures, strapwork, and such biblical scenes as were considered appropriate to a court room. In the east lunette a central circular frame contains Shadrach, Meshach and Abednego in the burning fiery furnace, flanked by pictures of Daniel in the lion's den and the Judgement of Solomon. The three plaques are linked by a scheme of strapwork incorporating large caryatid figures of Wisdom with her book and blindfolded Justice with her scales. Opposite, at the west end of the room, is another strapwork fantasia enclosing a plaque with a phoenix rising triumphant from the flames below an oval cartouche containing a bear-like animal, possibly a badger or 'brock' (said to be the badge of a local family, the Brookes). This plasterwork is of the early seventeenth century.

44. **Court House**, **Chard**
Court Room;
Below: *East Lunette, c.1620*
Bottom: *West Lunette, c.1620*

In sharp contrast to the magnificence of the Chard decorations, the little room above the porch of the **Old Manor House, Combe Florey**, has a unique decorative scheme of the late sixteenth century that encompasses the whole room *(fig. 106)*. Four fluted pilasters with an Elizabethan version of Ionic capitals occupy the corners, while the walls between are divided into regular panels, set lozenge-wise on one wall and square on the other, containing heraldic animals and Tudor badges. There are a boar, lions, a Tudor rose and portcullis, a stag's head and other motifs, the frieze above having a simple design of large-scale flowers with a leafy meander. The whole decoration of the room is orderly and typically Elizabethan in character.

Two decorative but isolated wall panels deserve mention here, if only for their singularity. In an upper chamber of the **Little Fort, Milverton**, proportioned much like pew ends, they depict in low relief a symmetrically-designed plant that is recognisably a Crown Imperial *(fig. 45)*. Where the panels came from and for what purpose they were made is unknown, but they were probably once part of a larger decorative scheme. The design is well executed and appears Jacobean in style, very comparable to embroidery patterns of the period.

45. **Little Fort, Milverton**
Chamber, wall panels, c.1600

21 H.C. Maxwell Lyte, *History of Dunster*, ii. 179; A. Oswald, 'Montacute Re-visited - III', *Country Life*, 3 November 1955.

22 *Somerset and Dorset Notes and Queries*, xviii. 278

23 *V.C.H. Somerset*, vi. 47-8

24 Information from the owner

25 Mary Buncombe succeeded to her sister's share of the manor in 1691 and died in 1706: *V.C.H. Somerset*, vi. 47.

26 Mr. Michael Snodin of the Victoria and Albert Museum confirmed the subject matter and the authors are indebted to him for his advice; the subject is fully set out in J. Hall, *Dictionary of Subjects and Symbols in Art*.

27 *Visitations of Somerset, 1623*, ed. Colby, 50, 110.

28 See page 7

29 *V.C.H. Somerset*, vi. 175

30 See page 25

31 Pedigree in *The Trevelyan Letters to 1840*, ed. M. Siraut (Somerset Record Soc. lxxx), pp. xiv-xv.

32 *V.C.H. Somerset*, vi. 81.

33 See page 14

46. **Priors Farm, Stringston**
Parlour, c.1650

CHAPTER 5

CRAFTSMEN

Further illustrations
are on pages 67 to 69

VERY LITTLE IS KNOWN about Somerset plasterers. It is believed that the great bulk of the work in the county, if not all, was executed by native craftsmen and not by foreigners, whether Italian or Flemish. The sheer quantity of plasterwork in Somerset makes the use of foreign craftsmen for all but a very small proportion of the work improbable. If they were working here in any numbers, it seems almost incredible that no record whatever of their employment has come to light.

Nevertheless, traditions to the contrary do persist. One is that the overmantels in **Court House, East Quantoxhead**, all highly accomplished, were made by a Flemish immigrant called Leversha, whose family subsequently stayed on in England as tenants on the Luttrell estate until modern times.[34] There is no known documentation to support or disprove the original Leversha having done the plasterwork, only the work itself, which shows a close affinity to some of Vredeman de Vries's patterns *(fig. 7)*.[35]

Another tradition, often heard, that plaster decorations were executed by 'Italian seamen who landed on the North coast' can be discounted. Quite apart from the inherent improbability of sailors carrying out plasterwork (presumably while waiting for a favourable wind to carry them home to the Mediterranean) the designs in the houses in question have more of the Flemish than the Italian in them - those Flemish-inspired patterns that had so caught the imagination of the Elizabethans and Jacobeans.

If, however, by native craftsmen, then who were they? There are only two known Elizabethan plasterers working in this part of the country; one a Somerset man, Robert Eaton of Stogursey, the other John Abbott and his family of Frithelstock in north Devon. Both Eaton and the elder John Abbott were working around 1600.

ROBERT EATON

Robert Eaton was working in **Combe Florey** in 1599, presumably in the manor house, for John Frauncis, who wrote on 13th September in that year to John Trevelyan at Nettlecombe Court, which was then nearing completion, to enquire when a certain Bartlett would finish his work at Nettlecombe: " ... the soner he hath don with you the glader shall I be for that *Robart Yeaton the plester man* cometh unto me this day and cannot worke longe before the chemley must be made, which I have a longe tyme exspected to be done by Bartlett ...".[36] So Eaton was to make an overmantel at Combe Florey and was waiting for the chimney to be built. He obviously had other work to do there, ceilings and friezes, perhaps. That has to remain speculative, since the sixteenth-century manor house has long since gone, but the fifteenth-century **Gatehouse** still stands. It has an excellently-designed and modelled late-Elizabethan overmantel *(fig. 47 & 114)*, frieze and ceiling in the upper chamber, the Tudor Room. The overmantel is dated 1593, six years before the date of the letter quoted above, so the Gatehouse was plastered some years before the house. Even so, it is reasonable to assume that the Gatehouse plasterwork was created by John Frauncis' 'plester man' Robert Eaton.

Eaton also worked in Dorset, where he carried out the interior decoration in the chapel at Chantmarle: the decoration of sun, moon, stars, cherubim, doves, grapes, pomegranates

47. **Gatehouse, Combe Florey**
Detail of overmantel, 1593

and angels " ... was wrought by Eaton of Stokegurzey or Stoye in Somersett and finished 2 Decembris 1615 ...".[37] But, once again, the building no longer stands and the plasterwork is lost.

Other work by Robert Eaton can only be identified on stylistic grounds. The overmantel in the Court Room at **Holcombe Court, Holcombe Rogus**, Devon *(fig. 115)*, echoes many of the design features seen in Combe Florey: the large rectangular frame surrounding the strapwork cartouche, the chubby faces of the supporting figures, the pot-bellied shield of arms and the sharply defined detail. Another chamber overmantel in the same house is of similar style and both are, in the opinion of the writers, by the same hand as the Combe Florey overmantel.

48. **Montacute House**
Hall chamber, c.1600

Six other houses, three in Somerset, one in Dorset and two in Devon, have plasterwork that can be linked stylistically together and with the work of Robert Eaton in Combe Florey and Holcombe Court. Three overmantels, in **Walronds, Cullompton**, 1605, **Weare Gifford Hall**, 1599, both in Devon, and in **Mapperton**, Dorset, 1604, the last named originally in Melplash Court, have the crisp efficiency of the style together with naked figures perched on the strapwork.

In Somerset, overmantels in the Oak Room, **Poundisford Lodge** *(fig. 105)*, 1590, the Great Chamber of the **Manor House, West Coker**, and three chamber overmantels in **Montacute House** *(fig. 48, 104 & 116)* have the same sort of figures. All share some of the similarities that go to make a recognisable style: rounded features framed in bonnets or hair; terms or caryatids carrying baskets or bunches of fruit on their heads with projecting cucumbers, which also distinguish the many fruit bunches hanging from the cartouches; the bulging armorial shields and many other minor features. There is a direct connection between Montacute and Combe Florey: in the Great Chamber of the **Manor House, West Coker** *(fig. 8)*, the overmantel is undoubtedly by the same hand as made the Montacute ones and the frieze is the same tulip design as that in Combe Florey. Attributing authorship by stylistic comparison cannot be positive proof but, taking Combe Florey as a starting point, it seems extremely likely that all this distinguished work is by Robert Eaton.

Very little is known about Robert Eaton. He married Grace Waterman at Stogursey in 1602 (she died in 1621) and, described as a yeoman, he leased a cottage in Stogursey with 20 perches of land for 14s. c.1614.[39] Where he was born and died has not yet been found, and it seems sad that so talented a craftsman should have such a brief obituary.

THE ABBOTTS

Of the various centres for plasterwork design in neighbouring Devon, the Barnstaple 'school', if it can be called that, appears the most closely linked with Somerset.

John Abbott the elder, of Frithelstock (1565-1635), his son Richard and his more celebrated grandson John the younger (1639-1727) worked as a family of plasterers and have left a sketch-book, now in the Devon Record Office, containing designs spanning almost 150 years of stylistic development. It was recovered from the descendants of John Abbott of Frithelstock soon after the Second World War and contains innumerable designs for plasterwork, drawn out in varying degrees of competence. Many of those designs for ceilings and overmantels have been identified in Devon houses by Cecil and Kathleen French[40] and by Margaret Jourdain.[41] The example of most interest to this study is the 'Triumph of Time'.[42] This scene, sketched very roughly in the book, is recognisable in its main elements as the design for the centre-piece of the overmantel in **Dean Head, Swimbridge**, Devon, which has therefore been attributed to the Abbotts *(fig. 118)*. The same scene executed in the same high relief but with a few more foreground figures, rather better modelled and facing the other way, is seen at **Binham Farm, Old Cleeve**, Somerset *(fig. 117)*. In spite of treating the same subject, there are enough well-marked dissimilarities between the Dean Head Triumph and the Binham one to say that they are by different hands. In Dean Head the modelling is weaker, the grouping and composition more primitive and the whole concept, with its strapwork background, is quite unlike its more sophisticated counterpart in Binham Farm.

49. **Marshwood Farm, Carhampton**
Porch, 'Naboth's Vineyard'

In the porch of **Marshwood Farm, Carhampton**, the Naboth's Vineyard overmantel *(fig. 49)*, in which similar high relief figures can be recognised, is almost certainly by the same craftsman as the Binham Farm example, as is the Abraham and Isaac which faces the

Vineyard across the porch at Marshwood *(fig.36)*. The only other Somerset example of work in this genre is, of course, the best known of all, the Skimmington Ride in **Montacute House**. All these scenes tell a story, all have figures in seventeenth-century dress, all are competently executed and the Naboth's Vineyard and the Montacute scene are both designed like strip cartoons with different events shown in the same picture.

There is, however, another pair of overmantels which share a common authorship. The overmantel in the **Luttrell Arms, Dunster** *(fig. 119)*, is, no doubt at all, by the same craftsman who made the one in **no. 18 Fore Street, Taunton** *(fig. 120)*; the caryatids are identical and there are clear similarities in the fruit bunches and strapwork. Although not identical, the caryatids in these examples are so like the ones in Binham Farm, especially their faces, as to suggest that the plasterwork in Binham Farm, the Luttrell Arms, 18 Fore Street, Marshwood Farm and, finally, the Montacute Skimmington Ride can all be grouped together as the work of one plasterer or family of plasterers working in the early seventeenth century.

It must be remembered that Robert Eaton 'of Stogursey' presumably based his business there and that all the examples quoted here with the exception of Montacute lie within 15 miles of it. It is doubtful if the name of the craftsman responsible for the work will ever be known for certain. It is just possible that it was Eaton; it seems less likely that it was the Abbotts, since Frithelstock lies some 50 miles away to the west.

OTHER CRAFTSMEN

Identification by stylistic comparison of the work of named craftsmen such as Eaton or the Abbotts is obviously more satisfactory than doing the same thing with anonymous ones. Nevertheless there is a remarkable quartet of houses which contains early seventeenth-century plasterwork of a unique and unmistakable character, all carried out with great assurance and imagination. There is little doubt that all four are by the same, as yet unidentified, craftsman.

50. **Wigborough Manor, South Petherton**
Parlour ceiling

The houses in question are **Weston Farm, Wambrook**; **Court House, Chard**; **Wigborough Manor, South Petherton** *(fig. 50)*, and **Whitestaunton Manor**. In the early seventeenth century the Bonner family of Weston Farm were linked by marriage with the Comptons of Wigborough and all four houses lie not far apart in south Somerset. Plasterwork in three of them can be dated by coats of arms commemorating marriages: Weston Farm *c.*1614, Wigborough *c.*1628 and Whitestaunton *c.*1630. The plasterwork in Court House cannot be similarly dated but Thomas Gerard, writing in 1633, speaks of the buildings there as being 'much amended':[43] the date seems quite compatible with the style of the work and fits in well enough with the other dates.

The most obvious characteristics of the designs, common to all four examples, are the choice of strange animals and monsters, the treatment of the human head, round and with the eyes high up in the forehead, and a tendency to mould flat surfaces in strapwork, foliage, wings, etc. with a pronounced concavity. Identical animal forms appear in three of the four.

Weston Farm is the earliest and the most extreme design, with an overpowering presence of weird and sinister creatures. **Whitestaunton Manor** Chamber frieze echoes some of the Weston Farm creatures and exhibits all the characteristics of the style. The **Wigborough** Parlour plasterwork has the faces and animals of the other two, although the ceiling detail is on a smaller scale, while the much larger designs of the **Court House**, besides showing the characteristics of the style, incorporate at least one of the creatures seen at Weston Farm *(fig. 121, 122, 123 & 124)*. No other comparable work has yet been found in Somerset.

It is hardly surprising that minor work, however competent, in small farms or even manor houses should pass undocumented, but in great houses it is strange that the enormous sums of money that must have been spent on the huge, richly wrought ceilings of the classical period of the Civil War and after are not apparently recorded. **Forde Abbey**, Dorset, which has rather too many Red Indians and creatures with a Jacobean flavour to qualify as pure sophisticated classicism, is mid-century work, possibly executed by a local craftsman familiar with classical design. **Halswell House, Goathurst** *(fig. 79)* and **Dunster Castle** *(fig. 21 & 78)*, however, have huge ceilings covered in sumptuous plasterwork in the fully developed style of the 1680s. It is at least possible that they were both executed by London craftsmen rather than local men. Edward Goudge, a famous master craftsman with a national reputation, has been suggested as being responsible for the work at Dunster.[44]

34 The authors are indebted to Col G.W.F. Luttrell for telling them about this tradition.

35 See page 7

36 S.R.O., Trevelyan MSS., DD/WO 56/4. We owe this reference to Dr R.W. Dunning

37 Dorset Record Office, Strode MSS. MW/MA.

38 Arthur Oswald, writing in *Country Life* (3 November 1955), makes very similar comparisons and relates the designs to the master mason William Arnold, under whose direction the plasterer is presumed to have worked. Cecil French amplified this article in his letter to *Country Life* (8 December 1955). It is resonable to assume that a master mason would employ the same craftsman on many projects, in this case, the writers believe, Robert Eaton.

39 S.R.O., D/P/stog 2/1/1; ibid. DD/X/WI 34.

40 *The Countryman*, liii. no. 4 (Winter 1956)

41 *Country Life*, March 1940.

42 See page 34

43 *The Particular Description of the County of Somerset* (Somerset Record Society xv), 72.

44 G. Beard, *The English House Interior*, 111-12

51. **No 18 Fore Street, Taunton**
*Chamber, c.1620, showing
ceiling, overmantel and frieze*

CHAPTER 6

TECHNIQUE *and* CONSERVATION

THIS CHAPTER IS DEVOTED to a general review of the plastering technique of the sixteenth and seventeenth centuries as revealed by close inspection of surviving work, more particularly by experience gained in restoration and by careful analysis of fragments recovered during repairs. Much of this early practice is the same as that used within living memory, the only changes in basic technique being those brought about by new materials. Expert plaster craftsmen intimately concerned with the conservation and restoration of traditional decorative plasterwork in the West Country have been consulted.[45]

BACKING

Before plastering could start, a suitable background had to be prepared. On solid walls this consisted of little more than seeing that the stone and brickwork was rough enough and the joints sufficiently raked out to provide a good grip for the undercoat. For timber ceilings and partitions, where plaster rather than wattle and daub was used, lathing was necessary. Timber studs in walls and joists in floors were normally spaced 12" to 18" apart and lathing was provided to span between. Split wooden laths of oak or chestnut were nailed to the timbers to form a continuous flat surface leaving a gap between each lath so that the plaster could squeeze in between. The resulting 'key' was what held the plaster in place. Oak and chestnut were chosen because they were straight grained and split easily. The timber was best used green, unseasoned, so that being slightly damp it was less likely to be warped by the wet process and did not take the moisture out of the plaster too quickly.

In Somerset, where the moors and wetlands provided an ample supply of water reed, reed-lath was commonly used instead of split timber. The reeds were applied in a continuous layer fixed with timber laths nailed through the reeds along each joist or stud. Generally, reed lasts better than split timber as it is less liable to insect and fungus attack. Although apparently not so strong as timber, it has been successfully used as backing for fully decorated ceilings of very considerable thickness and weight. (All the elaborately decorated seventeenth-century plasterwork in Barrow Court, Barrow Gurney, is supported on reed lath).

PLASTER

The plaster itself was made of sand and lime with various aditions, especially hair. Stucco duro (Chapter 1) was for the most part only used by Italian craftsmen doing special work for royalty or the aristocracy, and gypsum or Plaster of Paris for fine work does not seem to have been used until the high-relief elaborations of classical decoration became fashionable after the Civil War, when a little of the material may have been added to the mix to accelerate the set in enrichments. This was done possibly in the plasterwork of Forde Abbey and probably in that of Dunster Castle.

Sand is plentiful in Somerset and presented no problems except that sea sand could never be used as the salts would dry out as a furry white efflorescence and the work would be spoiled. Lime was made from limestone, the stone being first crushed and then burnt in a kiln. Any limestone can be suitable for making lime; in Somerset the Blue Lias from the Lower Lias beds was much used. The burnt lime was 'slaked' by adding water which caused it to bubble and boil until all its caustic quality had been removed. The slaked lime was then stored for as long as possible, even for as long as a year, so that no minute particles remained unslaked to cause subsequent bubbles or blows in the plasterwork. The resulting lime putty was mixed with sand in varying proportions, less lime being required in undercoats and rather more in finishing coats and decorations, a normal proportion for the latter being four parts of sand and one part of lime.

The plaster was applied to the backing in one or more rough undercoats and finished in finer material with one, sometimes two, top coats. The undercoats were made of very coarse material, not unlike the daub used for wattle-and-daub partitions but with added lime and hair. The resilience and toughness of the undercoat seems to have been much improved by the addition of all sorts of impurities such as brick dust, dung or grit. Large quantities of hair were beaten into the mix to give the plaster tensile strength. The hair, which is rot-resistant and seems to last for ever, was usually red ox or cow hair, probably obtained from tanneries or the spring clippings of the draught oxen. The top or finishing coat in decorative work was a skim coat applied very thinly between the decorations. In ribbed ceilings the skim coat was applied after the ribs had been formed.

The material for a thin skim coat was probably pure lime, but even so with fine hair beaten into the mix, in this case goat's or kid's hair, so thin it can hardly be seen. In less refined top coats and in most enrichments the mix was made of lime and fine sand with white ox-hair.

DECORATIONS

Ribs on ceilings were applied direct to the undercoat, the pattern being marked out first on the under surface of the ceiling. They were formed by applying plaster to the pattern and running back and forth with a horse or template cut to the profile of the moulded rib. Double ribs and wide ribs were made in the same way and, in the case of enriched ribs, it seems that the floral or other pattern was sometimes stamped into wet plaster placed between the ribs, using a mould like a butter-pat. At intersections where the horse could not be run, the ribs were made good by hand, the less precise mouldings that resulted usually covered by four plaster leaves or a small boss. Cornices were similarly run with a horse, fashioned to the required profile, and the corners were again done by hand.

Enrichment like floral sprays, fleurs-de-lis or other motifs on ceilings and friezes were either modelled by hand in situ using fingers and modelling spatulas or, if small, stamped with a mould. On later repetitive work, decorations were more often cast in moulds and, when set, stuck to the wall or ceiling with wet plaster.

Some friezes were moulded by hand, but the generality of the repetitive patterns were cast in moulds. The patterns were designed in lengths appropriate to the depth of the frieze; the narrower the frieze the shorter the repeat pattern, so that the resulting cast panels were not too long and thin for safe handling, for such work was cast on the ground and fixed up into place in sections. The length of repeat and the joins between sections in friezes can be clearly seen, the joins sometimes rather roughly done.

52. **No. 3 Cork Street**, **Frome**
A modern plaster cast of a seventeenth century frieze

MOULDS

Moulds were made from fine-grained wood such as yew, beech or fruit wood. Casts were taken from the moulds before the set had fully hardened and were titivated by hand to achieve undercuttings and drillings, some retarder such as fruit juice being sometimes added to the mix to slow down the setting and to give the craftsman more time for this sort of work.

Early Elizabethan overmantels comprising simple arrangements of formal mouldings such as those at **Higher Southtown Farm, West Pennard**, and in **Mapperton, Dorset**, were cast from moulds (indeed, in these two particular houses the same mould was used), but the elaborate and varied overmantel designs of the 1590s and later, often in high relief and with figures virtually in the round, did not lend themselves to casting and were invariably modelled by hand.

ARMATURES

Cornices, decorative brackets, figures and large panels need an internal structure or armature on which to build up the design. This was made of wood with laths or with willow sticks. Cornices were bracketed out from wall and ceiling, and longitudunal runners were added and roughly clad in lathing before running the mouldings.

In late seventeenth-century and early eighteenth-century work, where realistic leaves and flowers in three dimensions were used in the design, each individual leaf or flower was separately made, using an armature of copper wire or twigs, and was individually stuck up by hand, a most elaborate and laborious task on a large, high-class ceiling. Pendants, where small, were made of solid plaster but the larger pendants had a timber core bolted up to the joists and all major pendants had a central rod terminating in a ring from which to hang a lamp or candelabrum. One large pendant in the Hall at Poundisford Park appears to be entirely made of turned wood, but this was not normal sixteenth-century practice. Where plaster was taken across timber boards or wide beams the surface of the wood was crudely hacked all over with an axe to make rough slits into which the plaster could hold. Where the work was exceptionally heavy, nails could be used, hammered in to hold the undercoat.

COLOUR

In contrast to the Tudor fashion for mural decoration and painted timber beams, colour seems not to have been used on moulded plasterwork until well on in the eighteenth century. This view is not generally held, but it is based on a wide practical experience of conservation work in the West Country. Tudor wall and ceiling paintings on timber and plaster were essentialy flat-surface embellishments. Perhaps the new technique of making raised patterns in plaster was regarded as an alternative to colour, welcome in its whiteness as making the most of the airy, well-lit interiors that resulted from the huge fashionable windows. This state of affairs seems to have lasted until the Civil War, but by the last half of the seventeenth century gilding began to be used to enrich still further the overpowering classical decorations of the period. (Before the Civil War gilding was only used in the grandest of buildings like the Banqueting House in Whitehall).

Even on coats of arms, where it is an important point of identification, colour seems not initially to have been used. In one Devon example, finely-grooved hatching to represent the different tints took the place of colour, but generally the various motifs that go to make the shield patterns were allowed to stand on their own. The colouring of coats of arms is usually a later improvement. In the mid eighteenth century pastel-coloured backgrounds became fashionable following the introduction of Pompeian designs by the Adam Brothers, but prior to that all ordinary plasterwork was probably left white.

CONSERVATION

Conservation implies preserving and where necessary rescuing what is there and accepting it as an old piece of craftsmanship that is none the worse for looking its age. Where rescue is required, conservation techniques are a matter of knowledge and experience, of ingenuity and skill and, of course, of the availability of the proper tools and equipment.

Other than simple preventative precautions, work should never be undertaken by the householder without proper advice. Conservation is different from restoration, which implies making good all defects and replacing all missing parts, the intention being to reproduce a piece of workmanship that is as good as new. Needless to say there are occasions when restoration is entirely justified as, for instance, when a great house is gutted and rebuilt. Many Wren churches in London, destroyed in the war, have been most beautifully restored and no one can deny the effort was worthwhile. But such major disasters apart, conservation is more concerned with not allowing detioration to go so far that the work cannot be rescued, for it is the preservation of the actual pieces of material fashioned by hand so long ago that is important. That such a fragile material, supported on thin laths or reeds, should have lasted in such quantity and for so long in domestic premises that have suffered the ups and downs of fortune over the centuries, is something of a miracle. This is due to the use of robust materials that seem to be able to take a great deal of punishment, also to the excellence of the craftsmanship; and again to the enduring materials of which the houses themselves are built and to their capacity for permanence and for remaining weatherproof under all and every changing circumstance.

Those fortunate enought to own decorative plasterwork should give it as good a chance of continuing survival as they can and there are certain simple preventative measures that can be taken towards that end. Other than looking after the general fabric of the house and keeping it in good repair, perhaps the first rule is to leave well alone. As in all antique survivals, when the work is in reasonably good condition and shows no signs of distress, it is best left to look after itself.

Next is the realisation of how plasterwork is made and all that that implies. Ceilings are held up on lathing which is nailed to the ceiling joists. The plaster is heavy and laths and nails are old and fragile, so never allow any hammering on the floor above. The introduction of heating pipes creates local hot spots which are very bad for plasterwork and its support;

they should never be run in the void above old ceilings. When builders, plumbers or electricians are working in the house they must be kept as far as possible away from areas where there is plasterwork below, or they must be asked to proceed wih extreme caution, using screws rather than nails and avoiding causing vibration as far as they can.

In regard to decoration, if the plasterwork really does have to be painted, never use modern emulsion or vinyl paints and of course never use gloss paints. All these are much too strong for what is underneath. Limewash is the traditional material and an excellent *Information Sheet* on the subject, written by Jane Schofield, has been published by the Society for the Protection of Ancient Buildings (S.P.A.B.), describing various methods of preparation. Proprietory 'Limewhite' can be purchased ready made.

Where the decorations are really smothered in layers of old paint or whitewash, cleaning can be a worthwhile improvement, but this should not be attempted without first getting proper advice; different sorts of paint need different treatments. Contact the Conservation Officer at County Hall, Taunton, and ask for advice; or ask S.P.A.B. to help. It is possible that they may recommend a course of treatment that can be carried out by the owner himself, or they may suggest that the work should be done by a professional conservator.

Split timber laths and wooden armatures (and to a lesser extent reeds) get eaten away by woodworm and beetle larvae, leaving a plaster ceiling hanging below the joists, apparently unsupported, held up by the tensile strength in the plaster itself. Under such extreme (but alas not infrequent) circumstances the bulging and cracking of the ceiling is soon apparent. Similarly friezes, especially on timber partitions, can crack and begin to fall away, and overmantels can suffer from accidental knocks and the gradual deterioration of the underlying framework. All this presents a daunting picture, but even if deterioration has gone so far, help and expert advice is at hand. Keep the pieces that fall away and call for help; conservators can work wonders of reinstatement and the County Conservation Officer or the S.P.A.B. will advise on specialist contractors and on possible grants to help pay for the work of rescue.

53. No. 3 Cork Street, Frome
The repaired frieze

---

45 David Hayles of Hayles and Howe, Plasterers, of Bristol, and Jane Schofield, Plasterwork Conservator, both of whom are experts in their field.

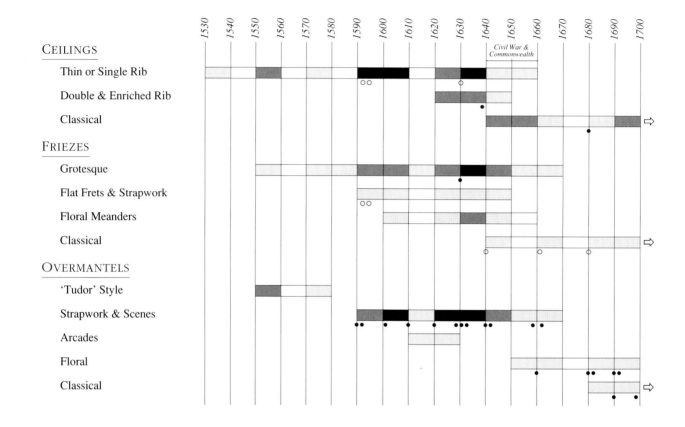

CEILINGS
    Thin or Single Rib
    Double & Enriched Rib
    Classical

FRIEZES
    Grotesque
    Flat Frets & Strapwork
    Floral Meanders
    Classical

OVERMANTELS
    'Tudor' Style
    Strapwork & Scenes
    Arcades
    Floral
    Classical

CHRONOLOGICAL RANGE OF PRINCIPAL DESIGN FEATURES

■	More than 4 examples per decade
▨	3 or 4 examples per decade
░	1 or 2 examples per decade
•	Dated examples
○	By association with dated overmantels

SUMMARY

IT IS CUSTOMARY to attempt to draw conclusions from a study of this sort or at least to summarise. To do so it is necessary to stand back a little from the plethora of detail and to look at the general picture.

In the west and south of the 1974 administrative county of Somerset, decorative plasterwork is similar in character to that in neighbouring Devon and to a lesser extent to that in Dorset. All three counties share a strong tradition of plasterwork design. A good deal has been written about Devon plasterwork and emphasis has been given to the Exeter and Barnstaple 'schools', but whether Devon was the source of inspiration for Somerset plasterers or vice versa must remain a matter for speculation or local loyalties. Influence, in any case, is likely to have been a two-way traffic.

Elaborate late sixteenth- and early seventeenth-century overmantels with scenes in relief are typical for south-west Somerset and for Devon as are the well designed and executed ceilings, but Somerset itself is remarkable for the late Elizabethan and Jacobean caryatid figures in the round, more numerous and for the most part better modelled than their counterparts in Devon.

In the north-east of the county the style changes. Here plasterwork is seen to be generally rather later in date and there is a change of emphasis from huge overmantels to smaller and simpler designs, and from overall to central ceiling patterns. The rich farming country around Taunton and south Somerset seems to have generated more prosperity somewhat earlier, and at a wider range of social levels than in the north-east where it is likely that the wealth created by the woollen cloth industry may have been concentrated in fewer hands.

It is probable that virtually all Somerset plasterwork was executed by native craftsmen, the overmantels of Court House, East Quantoxhead, being the most likely exception. One Somerset plasterer working c.1600 is known by name, Robert Eaton of Stogursey. It appears that he was responsible for a good deal of high quality work in the area.

The chart on page 52 showing the chronological distribution of Somerset examples indicates a peak period of activity from 1590 to 1640, during which single-rib ceilings, grotesque friezes and strapwork overmantels predominate.

To attempt some final generalisations: the earliest ceiling designs looked to late-medieval architecture for inspiration and in only one case to Italianate sources. By contrast, late sixteenth- and early seventeenth-century frieze design is almost always of Italianate grotesque origin whereas the design of overmantels, right up to the Civil War, looks unwaveringly towards Flanders, with an overwhelming emphasis on Flemish-inspired strapwork. By the end of the Civil war, although the smaller houses continued to be built in the vernacular tradition of the preceding hundred years, interior design at all social levels had leapt the gap to embrace the ponderous formality of Italianate classicism. To assess at what moment this change occurred cannot by the nature of things be realistic, but transitional examples of the 1640s indicate that the Civil War can be regarded as a useful watershed.

54. **Yarde Farm, Staplegrove**

ILLUSTRATIONS

55. Ceiling Patterns

The dense-packed designs of the sixteenth century, the more open patterns of around 1600 and the opulent double and enriched ribs of the first half of the seventeenth century;

a: *Lytes Cary, Charlton Mackrell*

b: *Poundisford Park, Pitminster*

c: *Gate House, Combe Florey*

d: *Orchard Wyndham, Williton*

e: *Bell House, Milverton*

f: *Poundisford Lodge, Pitminster*

g: *No 18 Fore Street, Taunton*

h: *Court House, Chard*

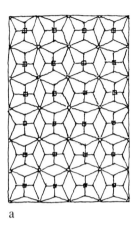

a

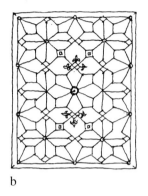

b

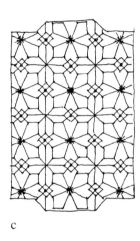

c

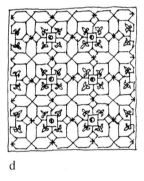

d

e

f

g

h

**Plaster Ceilings derived
from Fan Vaulting**

56. **Mapperton, Dorset**
The Great Chamber, c.1550

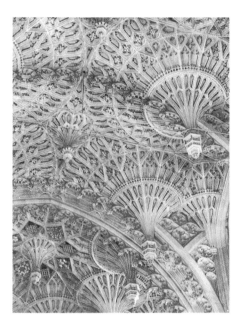

left: 57. **Henry VII's Chapel,
Westminster**; *Fan vaulting*

right: 58. **Barrow Court,
Barrow Gurney, Avon**
Staircase, seventeenth century?

59. **Poundisford Park,
Pitminster**; *Hall, c.1570*

Large scale, thin-rib Patterns

60. **Poundisford Lodge, Pitminster**; *Chamber, 1590*

left: 61. **Nutcombe Manor, Devon**; *Hall, c.1620*

right: 62. *Pattern from 'A Booke of Sundry Draughts' by Walter Gedde, published 1615*

Double Rib Ceilings

63. **The Court House, Chard**
Court Room, barrel ceiling and lunette, c.1620 (after drawing by W. Bidgood, 1883 SANHS Proc.)

WALL AND CEILING, IN MANOR COURT HOUSE, CHARD.— East End.

Double Rib Ceilings

left: 64. **Weston Farm, Wambrook**; *Parlour, c.1620*

right: 65. **Hinton House, Hinton St George** *State Dining Room, inscribed date 1636*

Plasterwork in the Frome area

66. **Glebe House, Great Elm** *Chamber, c.1630*

67. **Manor Cottages, Laverton, Lullington**; *Chamber lunette and cage pendant, c.1630*

68. **Manor Farm House, Laverton, Lullington**; *Hall, c.1627*

**Strapwork designs and
a Floral Spray**

69. **Beckington Abbey**
Great Chamber, c.1640

left: 70. **Beckington Abbey**
Detail of coved cornice

right: 71. **Plud Farm,
Stringston**; *Large floral spray,
probably mid seventeenth
century*

Pendants

72. **Nettlecombe Court**
*Hall, early seventeenth century
enriched rib*

Pendants

left: 73. **Poundisford Park**,
Pitminster; *Hall, c.1570*

right: 74. **Barrow Court**,
Barrow Gurney, Avon
Staircase, seventeenth century?

Oval wreaths

75. **Gaulden Manor, Tolland**
Hall, c.1640

left: 76. **Bournes**,
Wiveliscombe;
Parlour, c.1650

right: 77. **Nettlecombe Court**
Chamber, c.1640

Ornate Classical Ceilings

left: **78. Dunster Castle**
Dining Room, 1681

right: **79. Halswell House,
Goathurst**; *Chamber,
c.1690 (restored)*

80. Forde Abbey, Dorset
Dining Room, c.1655

Naturalistic Modelling, c.1700

81. Farm Estate, Fiddington
Parlour

Naturalistic Modelling, c.1700

left: 82. **Farm Estate,**
Fiddington; *Parlour, detail*

right: 83. **Nettlecombe Court**
Parlour, detail

Grotesque Friezes

84. **Poundisford Park,**
Pitminster; *Gallery, c.1570*

85. **Poundisford Park,**
Pitminster; *Hall, c.1570*

86. **Haddon Hall, Derbyshire**
second half of the sixteenth
century; compare with
Poundisford Park

87. **Orchard Wyndham,**
Williton; *Peacock chamber,*
c.1600

Narrow Friezes

88. Beckington Abbey
Great Chamber, c.1640

89. Priors Farm, Stringston
Parlour (overmantel dated 1658)

90. Gatehouse, Combe Florey
Tudor Room, 1593

91. Court House, Chard
The Court Room, c.1620

**92. Yea Cottage, Cushuish,
Cothelstone**
*Hall, Monkey Frieze, early
seventeenth century*

Thin-stemmed Friezes

**93. The Croft, Washford,
Old Cleeve**; *Hall, probably
early seventeenth century*

94. Dunster Castle and
Nutcombe Manor, Devon
c.1620

Thin-stemmed Friezes

95. **The Gables,
Stoke-sub-Hamdon**
*(and other houses),
early seventeenth century*

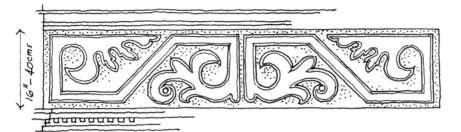

96. **Nettlecombe Court**
Parlour, c.1640

Deep Friezes

97. **Montacute House**
Crimson Room, c.1600

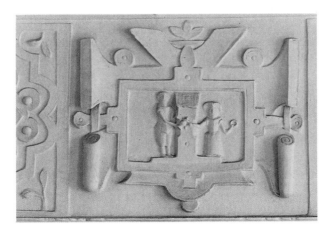

98. **Wigborough Manor,
South Petherton**
*Parlour, (figures at a well?),
c.1620*

99. **Montacute House**
Library, (flat frets), c.1600

Coats of Arms

100. Wigborough Manor,
South Petherton
Parlour, c.1630

101. Gaulden Manor, Tolland
Chamber, c.1640

102. Newton Surmaville,
Barwick; *Chamber, early*
seventeenth century

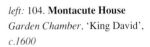

Scenes and Initials

103. **Parsonage Farm,**
Over Stowey
Chamber, 'Adam & Eve',
early seventeenth century

left: 104. **Montacute House**
Garden Chamber, 'King David',
c.1600

left: 105. **Poundisford Lodge,**
Pitminster; *Chamber, 1590*

Wall Decoration

right: 106. **Old Manor House,**
Combe Florey; *Porch Chamber,*
Elizabethan Ionic, c.1600

Unusual Designs

107. **Woodlands Farmhouse,**
Holford; *Chamber,*
'The Five Wounds of Christ',
mid seventeenth century?

108. **Old Bridge,**
South Petherton
Hall, 1665

Unusual Designs

**109. Chilton Trivet,
Cannington**; *Chamber, 1662*

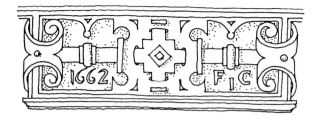

**110. The Corner House,
Alhampton, Ditcheat**
*Parlour, probably seventeenth
century*

Late Designs

**111. Steyning Manor,
Stogursey**; *Hall, c.1680*

**112. Elworthy Farmhouse,
Elworthy**; *Chamber, 1686*

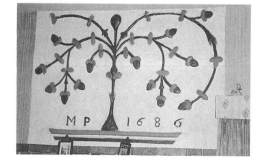

113. Church Close, Goathurst
Hall wall plaque, c.1690

Three overmantels - probably the work of Robert Eaton of Stogursey

114. **Gatehouse, Combe Florey**
Tudor Room, 1593

115. **Holcombe Court, Holcombe Rogus**, Devon
Court Room, 1591

116. **Montacute House**
Hall chamber, c.1600

'The Triumph of Time'
-two versions of the same subject, early seventeenth century

117. Binham Farm, Old Cleeve

118. Dean Head,
Swimbridge, Devon

A comparison of similar Caryatids, c.1620

below: **119. The Luttrell Arms, Dunster**

below right:
120. No 18 Fore Street, Taunton; *(note similar frieze in Binham Farm*

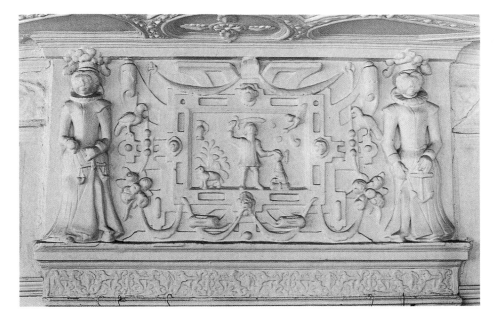

An Unknown Craftsman:
weird animals and
concave modelling

left: 121. **Wigborough Manor,
South Petherton**
overmantel, c.1630

right:
122. **Whitestaunton Manor**
*The Great Chamber Frieze,
plumed serpent, c.1630*

left: 123. **The Court House,
Chard**; *East lunette,
'Daniel in the Lions' Den', c.1620*

right:
124. **Weston Farm, Wambrook**;
Parlour ceiling, c.1620

GAZETTEER

ENTRIES ARE LISTED alphabetically under Civil Parishes and are numbered to correspond with the Distribution Map. Each entry is followed by references to text and illustrations (in italics). Points of the compass are indicated by initials only. Houses open to the public are marked with an asterisk(*). The privacy of all other properties should be respected.

DISTRIBUTION MAP

ASHILL

1 ■ **Rowlands**. Hall: *overmantel*, Royal Arms of Elizabeth I in enriched lozenge between thin pilasters with cornice and motto. *Frieze*, grotesque with unique lettering beneath, all round the room, e.g. TRUST IN GOD AND ABYDE IN THY PLACE ... PRESYNCE OF THE LORD MAKETH MEN RICH ... late C16. (Frieze and enriched lozenge are from the same moulds as those used in Poundisford Park, PITMINSTER, *c*.1570). Parlour: *ceiling*, isolated motifs, Tudor roses and fleurs-de-lis, from former barrel ceiling in Chamber, late C16. *(page 32)*

AXBRIDGE

2 ■ **St Jude's**, No 15 High Street. Rear Parlour: *frieze*, a simple meander of tulips alternately inverted (cf. Gatehouse, COMBE FLOREY, 1593). Rear Chamber: a narrow *frieze*, floral meander, part restored. All late C16 or early C17 and much obscured.

BARRINGTON

3 ■ ***Barrington Court**. Chamber (Solomon Room): small *overmantel*, Ionic columns on bases with paterae flanking simple strapwork cartouche with circular plaque and *scene*, Judgement of Solomon (I Kings 3); entablature above with running spirals, fruit and flowers, *c*.1630. (cf. CURRY MALLET Manor, Chamber). Chamber (Master Bedroom): *overmantel*, 3 rectangular painted panels (perhaps timber), central panel with shield of arms, Strode and Barnard (William Strode married Joan Barnard 1621 and bought Barrington in 1625: S. R. O. DD/HWY 9c/1134; *V.C.H. Somerset*, iv. 114).

BARWICK

4 ■ **Newton Surmaville**. Parlour: *ceiling*, thin-rib with floral sprays, face-mask bosses and small pendant, early C17. Chamber over Dining Room: *overmantel*, achievement of arms of the Harbin family, crest cut off by ceiling, vine trail border, early C17 (Frieze C19). Justice Room: fragment of early C17 *frieze* in cupboard (ceiling C19). *(page 15; fig. 102)*

BECKINGTON

5 ■ **Beckington Abbey**. Great Chamber: *ceiling* and *frieze*, unique in Somerset; a dramatic three-centred barrel covered in flat strapwork above a grotesque frieze and a deeply coved cornice; three pendants. The *cornice* and the *lunette* also covered in strapwork, all decorated with paterae, fleurs-de-lis, pomegranates, etc. *c*.1640. Chamber: *ceiling*, plain thin-rib stellar pattern, no leaf bosses or other motifs, C17. *(page 16, 18, 24; fig. 69, 70, 88)*

6 ■ **The Grange**. Formerly part of the Abbey. *Ceilings*: re-used C17 motifs in recent thin-rib designs.

7 ■ **The Old Manse**. Chamber: *ceiling*, two diagonally-set square panels either side of a beam, each with a crowned lion holding a rose bush with floral sprays and pomegranates; loose vine trails around the main panels. NE Chamber: *overmantel*, a simple rectangular panel supported on satyr masks containing two fleurs-de-lis, a thistle in an arch, the initials I W and the date 1670. *(page 35; fig. 40)*

8 ■ **Seymours Court**. Parlour: *ceiling*, two panels divided by an enriched plaster beam, each with similar four-petal thin-rib pattern with elaborate floral sprays in corners. *Frieze* (also on sides of beam), grotesque with plain shields (the same mould as for the Laverton friezes dated 1627, see LULLINGTON). All early or mid C17.

BISHOPS LYDEARD

9 ■ **Manor Cottage, Lower Terhill** (formerly East Bagborough manor). Wing Parlour: *ceiling*, mid C17 classical oval wreath with wide bands decorated with frieze moulds as used in Priors Farm, STRINGSTON. *Frieze*, 'monkey' design grotesque, from moulds used in Yea Cottage, Cushuish, COTHELSTONE. *Overmantel* (painted), naive strapwork cartouche with achievement of arms flanked by caryatids, Hope and Wisdom, mid C17. Wing Chamber: *ceiling*, one large Tudor rose. *Overmantel*, square panel in strapwork *cartouche* with *scene*, Samson slaying the Philistines with the jawbone of an ass (Judges 15), flanked by pilasters with voluted caps, early C17.

BRYMPTON

10 ■ **Brympton d'Evercy House**. Drawing Room: *ceiling*, large central oval wreath of bay/laurel with ribbon binding. Continuous convex *frieze* of the same 'wreath' design similarly banded. Other rooms in S Wing: the same *frieze*. All *c*.1680.

11 ■ **The Priest's House**. Chamber: good *ceiling* with thin-rib petal pattern and pendant, floral sprays and leaf bosses. *Frieze*, floral meander, early C17.

CANNINGTON

12 ■ **Chilton Trivet Farm**. Parlour: *ceiling*, four plain panels between moulded and coved beams. Parlour Chamber: *ceiling*, exuberant, central floral design with knob pendant. *Overmantel*, late strapwork panel dated 1662 with initials F I C (Francis Cridland and wife: *V.C.H. Somerset* vi. 81). *Cornice* and pulvinated *frieze* with acanthus brackets, heavy experimental classical, mid to late C17. *(page 37; fig. 109)*

13 ■ **Gurney Manor**. Small first-floor landing in Solar Wing: thin-rib geometric *ceiling* with elaborate fleurs-de-lis in the panels, *c.*1600. Recently restored by the Landmark Trust.

CARHAMPTON

14 ■ **Marshwood Farm**, formerly part of the Luttrell estate; a house with excellent early C17 plasterwork. NE Parlour: *overmantel*, large coat of arms (Luttrell family), otter crest above, flanked by male terms with halberds. Porch: two large strapwork plaques, probably *overmantels* from elsewhere; E side *scene*, Naboth's Vineyard (I Kings 21); W side *scene*, Abraham and Isaac (Gen. 22) in small central octagon. Figures in both in Jacobean dress. Hall Chamber: *lunette* to plain barrel, thin spiral floral, central male figure flanked by deer. NW Chamber: *lunette*, part surviving, similar design with fish in central oval cartouche. *Overmantel*, strapwork with coat of arms (Luttrell impaling Popham) flanked by female caryatids holding ropes of fruit (Thomas Luttrell married Jane Popham 1621: Maxwell Lyte, *Hist. Dunster*, i. 179). Above modern ceilings, broken remnants of two further *lunettes*. *(page 26, 32, 43; fig. 36, 49)*

CHARD

15 ■ **Court House**. Court Room: a magnificent display. *Ceiling*, a large barrel covered in flat double-rib stellar patterns with sun, moon, stars, animals, etc., and one pendant with cherubs. *Frieze*, late grotesque foliated meander with acorns and dogs' heads. *Lunettes*; W, flat strapwork (*overmantel* incorporated) with phoenix as central feature; E, flat strapwork with three *scenes* in frames, Judgement of Solomon (I Kings 3), Shadrach, Meshach and Abednego in the Furnace (Dan. 3. 20) and Daniel in the Lions' Den (Dan. 6); two female caryatids, Justice and Wisdom. All early C17, repaired 1960s. *(page 17, 26, 38, 44; fig. 44, 55, 63, 91, 123)*

16 ■ **No 9 Fore Street**. Ground and first floor front rooms: *ceilings*, thin-rib geometrical with leaf bosses. First floor back room: ditto with *frieze* painted black, grotesque with masks, all late C16.

CHARLTON MACKRELL

17 ■ ***Lytes Cary**. Great Chamber in S Wing: earliest plaster *ceiling* in county, a three-sided barrel, thin-rib stellar pattern with Lyte and Horsey shields and Tudor roses (John Lyte married Edith Horsey 1521: Dunning, *Some Somerset Country Houses*, 84). *Lunette*, shield of arms of Henry VIII flanked by Tudor roses and fleurs-de-lis. The wing was built in 1533 and the plasterwork is considered contemporary. *(page 14; fig. 10, 12, 55)*

COMBE FLOREY

18 ■ **Gatehouse**. Great Chamber (the Tudor Room): *ceiling*, thin-rib geometrical with face-mask bosses. *Frieze*, flat-fret tulip design, alternately inverted. *Overmantel*, magnificent achievement of arms of John Frauncis with inscription above and date 1593, flanked by a pair of terms, male and female each side. Plasterer, probably Robert Eaton of Stogursey. *(page 15, 25, 30, 41; fig. 34, 47, 55, 90, 114)*

19 ■ **Old Manor House**. Hall: *ceiling*, four panels between heavily moulded beams, each panel with central large Tudor rose, floral sprays and cherubs in the corners, early C17. Parlour Chamber: *overmantel*, rectangular panel with motifs, fleurs-de-lis, etc. Porch Chamber: *walls*, Ionic pilasters, panels with lions, boars, stag-heads, etc. *Frieze*, floral spirals. An unusual overall design for this small room, *c.*1600. *(page 39; fig. 106)*

COTHELSTONE

20 ■ **Yea Cottage, Cushuish**. Hall: *frieze*, grotesque 'monkey' pattern with gryphons, early C17. Chamber: *overmantel*, rectangular panel in late strapwork surround with coat of arms (Butcher's Guild of Exeter), initials R Y, I Y and date 1674, all flanked by small figures on pedestals. Fireplace lintel with 'monkey' *frieze* as Parlour, installed upside-down. *(page 25; fig. 92)*

CREECH ST MICHAEL

21 ■ **Coal Harbour, Ham**. Parlour: well moulded *ceiling*, oval wreath with central *scene*, Abraham and Isaac (Gen. 22), corner spandrels outlined with wide bands of fruit and flowers, mid C17. *Overmantel*, two acanthus brackets and later coat of arms, Merchant Adventurers of London, with supporting winged horses, initials R B M (Robert and Mary Bobbett: *V.C.H.* Somerset vi. 20) and date 1679 with motto GOD BE OUR DEFENCE. Chamber: earlier *ceiling*, four panels of double-rib stellar pattern with fleurs-de-lis and small shields. *Frieze*, grotesque with urns. *Overmantel*, arcade of three floral arches over urns of flowers, *c.*1620. (Cf. Ashe Farm, THORNFALCON, and Hankridge Farm, WEST MONKTON). *(page 19; fig. 11)*

CROSCOMBE

22 ■ **Laurel Cottage**, Long Street. Front Room: *ceiling*, deep beams forming four framed panels, each with simple moulded borders and an isolated central three-lobed motif of a fleur-de-lis flanked by two primitive leaf shapes. ?early C17.

CUCKLINGTON

23 ■ **Shanks House**, Long Lane. NW Parlour: ornate *ceiling* with circular panel, floral wreath and isolated motifs. Stair-case: *ceiling and wall panels*, the ceiling less elaborate than the Parlour, but with well executed wall decorations, including small portrait heads in the string course as in Crowcombe Court, CROWCOMBE. All early C18, thought to have been executed by a plasterer working under Nathaniel Ireson of Wincanton.

CURRY MALLET

24 ■ **Manor House**. Main Chamber: *overmantel*, naive Ionic columns flanking Tudor roses and strapwork cartouche with central fleurs-de-lis; vine trail architrave above. E Wing Chamber: *overmantel*, enriched rectangular frame with vine trail around central floral spray, fleurs-de-lis and other floral decorations. Early C17.

DITCHEAT

25 ■ **The Corner House, Alhampton**. Parlour: *frieze*, above the mantel-piece a row of birds and flowers, impressed. On the left a short length of deep frieze comprising three upright trees, each with four flowers, with leaf and flower motifs between, all impressed. Probably C17 but reminiscent of the late C19 Arts and Crafts Movement. Chamber: *overmantel*, a rectangular panel with fluted pilasters enclosing a large fleur-de-lis, the date 1624 and three small shields with initials M G and W G, the third shield with roughly scratched W W. *(fig. 110)*

DUNSTER

26 ■ ***Dunster Castle**. Inner Hall: Early C17 style thin-rib stellar *ceiling*; three pendants with face masks. *Overmantel*, rectangular panel with coat of arms, Luttrell impaling Hadley dated 1589, all coloured. King Charles's Chamber: *overmantel* with strapwork and central cartouche, The Judgement of Paris, under fruit garlands (Minerva looking rather masculine with spear and shield) flanked by terms and putti and man-in-the-moon motifs, dated 1620; all in rectangular panel. Gallery: *frieze*, floral scrolls and thin-stemmed spirals; two designs from same mould as used at EAST QUANTOXHEAD and in Nutcombe Manor, Clayhanger, Devon. Great Staircase: *ceiling*, a magnificent heavy classical design with hunting scene in the foliage and a classical cornice. Withdrawing Room and Dining Room: more splendid classical *ceilings* with many panels of fruit and flower wreaths and *friezes* with acanthus and fruit garlands. Dining Room ceiling dated 1681. *(page 20, 27, 45; fig. 21, 23, 30, 78, 94)*

27 ■ **The Luttrell Arms Hotel**. Chamber: a very fine *overmantel* of two stages; top, figure (?George Luttrell) under a pediment; bottom, a central oval with *scene*, Death of Actaeon, in strapwork surround flanked by female caryatids, *c.*1620. Coat of arms in another chamber, Luttrell impaling Capps (George Luttrell married Silvestra Capps 1622: Maxwell Lyte, *Hist.* Dunster, i. 178). Parlour: four-panel *ceiling* between cross beams, each panel with central flower motif, the sides of the beams with a fruit and flower meander. *(page 33, 44; fig. 38, 119)*

EAST QUANTOXHEAD

28 ■ **Court House**, notable for its many fine early C17 *overmantels* with coats of arms and New Testament *scenes* in strapwork surrounds, traditionally considered to be Flemish work. The Hall overmantel has flanking

soldiers, an achievement of arms of the Luttrells, initials G L for George Luttrell and the date 1629. Other overmantels throughout the house, some with flanking figures, some without, have biblical scenes; two earlier overmantels in the Wing, one dated 1614. Several rooms have *friezes* of floral spirals, but there are no decorated ceilings. *(page 33, 41; fig. 2, 7, 37)*

ELWORTHY

29 ■ **Elworthy Farm**. Chamber: *overmantel*, painted, a simple branching tree or strawberry plant with leaves and fruit, initials M P and the date 1686. *(fig. 112)*

EVERCREECH

30 ■ **Priory Cottage**, Church View. Parlour: above the large Elizabethan fireplace, as an *overmantel*, three fleurs-de-lis, the initials M B and H B and two very small masks. Chamber: above a small C16 fireplace, a Crown, flanked by initials E R (Elizabeth Regina) over a large Tudor rose, flanked by initials I S. In the splayed window jambs of the same room, the initials I G and E G. All letters in the house are in the same style, raised and bordered, ?late C16.

FIDDINGTON

31 ■ **Farm Estate**. Parlour: *ceiling*, large central circular wreath of fruit and flowers with outer ring of husks; corner spandrels with stiffly modelled putti, torsos emerging from flower heads in scrollwork. Centrally on each side of the room, either a grotesque mask or a tightly scrolled shield, c.1700. *(page 21; fig. 81, 82)*

FITZHEAD

32 ■ **Burrow Farm**. Parlour: *ceiling*, early Georgian oval with stiff leaf floral sprays in corners and a small cornice.

33 ■ **Meadow Gate**. Parlour: *overmantel* of odd motifs, crown, fleur-de-lis, Tudor roses, with narrow flat-fret *frieze*, grotesque with bold animals and half-shields, c.1600.

34 ■ **Washers**. Parlour: four-panel framed *ceiling*, each panel with wreath of husks and leaves and central sunflower, deeply coved classical cornice with acanthus leaves in each corner, wreaths painted. c.1700 (cf. Nettlecombe Court). *(page 21)*

FROME

35 ■ **No 3A and 3B Cork Street**. Chamber *ceiling*, single rib stellar pattern centre-piece, with hand-modelled and cast floral sprays. *Frieze*, good grotesque paired gryphons; a smaller mermaid frieze over the windows. All restored by Hayles and Howe 1992. Ground floor shop: *ceiling*, central petal-shaped quatrefoil with cast floral sprays with monster heads (cf. The Grange, Tytherington, SELWOOD). Early to mid C17. *(fig. 52, 53)*

GLASTONBURY

36 ■ *Abbey Gatehouse. E Chamber: *ceiling* in four panels between medieval beams, three panels with a central boss surrounded by a simple cruciform pattern of grapes and leaves, one panel with a corner spray; probably coeval with front bay window, dated 1639.

37 ■ *Tribunal. Ground floor rear room: *ceiling*, four panels between beams, each with single-rib central pattern with Tudor rose, fleurs-de-lis and floral sprays, c.1600.

GOATHURST

38 ■ **Church Close** (former manor house). Hall: *lunettes* of plain barrel, two coats of arms of Buncombe impaling Poulet (John Buncombe married Mary Poulet 1650: inf. from owner). Plasterwork, recently coloured, is in the William and Mary style with palm fronds, etc., c.1690, probably by the same plasterer as Halswell House. *(page 32; fig. 113)*

39 ■ **Halswell House**. A superb display of classical plasterwork, c.1690, in part restored following a fire of 1923. Staircase and NE Chamber: *ceilings*, central wreaths, floral with husks, palms, shields and cherub faces.

Friezes, winged cherub faces, birds and garlands of fruit and flowers. NW Chamber: *frieze*, a restless pattern of fronds and central shields. Drawing Room: *ceiling*, a freer, almost rococco design, with floral wreath and naturalistic scrolls. Justice Room: over the entrance door, positioned from elsewhere, *overmantel* with *scene* of Daniel in the Lions' Den (Dan. 6), flanked by splendid female caryatids, Justice and Mercy, c.1620. *(page 20, 45; fig. 79)*

GREAT ELM

40 ■ **Glebe House**, formerly the rectory house, contains strapwork in the form of narrow flat strips not seen elsewhere. Front Chamber: thin-rib and flat-strip *ceiling*, central feature petal pattern with central rose and large radiating leaves. Hand modelled leaves and floral sprays. Rear Chamber: *ceiling*, flat-strip central design, part missing; a square with semi-circles, corner sprays and large central flower. *Overmantel*, similar flat-strip strapwork in squares and arches with coat of arms of Robert Hodges, rector 1628-45 (*Somerset Incumbents*, ed. Weaver, 82), including Talbot crest. All c.1630. *(page 16; fig. 66)*

HALSE

41 ■ **Halsewater**. Hall: *ceiling*, four panels between beams with central roses and corner leaves. *Frieze*, small running grape and leaf meander, late C16 (cf. Lower Stowford, HALSE).

42 ■ **Lower Stowford**. Hall: *ceiling*, similar to Halsewater. *Frieze*, badly obscured floral scrolls. *Overmantel*, Tudor style batons set diagonally to form chevrons with large single leaves between. May be mid C16 or, more likely, c.1600.

HINTON ST GEORGE

43 ■ **Hinton House**. State Dining Room: *ceiling*, an elaborate Jacobean style double-rib design with strange animals and the date 1636 inscribed on a bird. A central plain oval cuts across the pattern, all very well executed. The Dining Room is in the early classical (Inigo Jones style) S Wing. *(page 17; fig. 65)*

HOLFORD

44 ■ **Castle of Comfort**. Chamber: *ceiling*, central rose with four floral sprays. *Overmantel*, a central shield with three hunting horns (the Dodington arms) dated 1655 with floral sprays on either side. Initials I C and A C below the shield, possibly for John Cordwent and his wife (*Somerset Protestation* Returns and Subsidy Rolls, 288).

45 ■ **Dodington Hall**, Wing built 1581. Wing Parlour: *frieze*, early C17, comprising a rather heavy running meander of leaves and fruit, including pomegranates, anthemions and fleurs-de-lis; many shields on rounded plaques showing Dodington and Sydenham arms. Sir Francis Dodington married Anne Sydenham, widow, c.1630 (Collinson, *Hist. Somerset*, iii. 518). A section of the E wall repaired.

46 ■ **Woodlands Farmhouse**. Wing Chamber: crammed into a corner of the room, an *overmantel* (fireplace blocked below) comprising a very simple strapwork cartouche with heavy side scrolls showing the Five Wounds of Christ (hands, feet and heart), a design not seen elsewhere in the county; the side wings considerably damaged. Perhaps 1630-40. *(fig. 107)*

HORTON

47 ■ **Horton Cross Farm**. Hall: *frieze* on two walls, tulip pattern with scrolls, the flowers alternately inverted (cf. Gatehouse, COMBE FLOREY). On central beam, a small thin-stemmed floral meander, early C17.

HUISH CHAMPFLOWER

48 ■ **West Combe Farm**. Parlour: *ceiling*, simple thin-rib mouldings; a large square with quadrant corners and plain inner circle with central 'rose'. *Canopy* over Entrance Door: a good hood on shaped brackets containing a large shell with small central mask, flanked by formal sprays, c.1700.

49 ■ **West Catford**. Very simple wall decoration, now fragmentary, above later flat ceiling, almost certainly *lunettes* from former barrels. Low-end Chamber: top, a vase with opposed cockatrices; a central row of stiff floral sprays and fleurs-de-lis, bottom, a crude royal coat of arms and, below the ceiling, the date 1679. Inner Room Chamber: a central roundel with radiating floral sprays; on opposite wall a fireplace with running floral meander surround and an *overmantel* with royal coat of arms flanked by floral sprays, similar to the low-end chamber

design. The date 1679, which goes with the crude coats of arms, seems far too late for the E-C17 style of the grotesque and floral designs in the lunettes. *(page 25; fig. 15, 27)*

ISLE ABBOTS

50 ■ **Brome House**. Hall Chamber: deep hand-moulded *frieze* in panels; flat floral designs between bearded heads above leafy sprays divided by plain moulded strips; very simple execution, incomplete. Low-end Chamber: *frieze*, narrower than that in the hall chamber, two alternating designs of flat frets divided by balusters, early C17.

51 ■ **Five Steps**. In the entrance hall, a fragment only of a floral *frieze*, early C17.

KINGSBURY EPISCOPI

52 ■ **Bladon Cottage**. Hall: between elaborately carved wainscot and plaster cornice moulding, a fragmentary narrow *frieze* comprising alternating simple fleurs-de-lis and flowers (Tudor rose and daisy) spaced at intervals to correspond with wainscot pilasters, *c*.1600-20.

LULLINGTON

53 ■ **Manor Cottages, Laverton**. Wing Chamber, S end: *barrel ceiling*, lost above late bedroom ceiling; an enriched-rib petal pattern and a large central cage *pendant* decorated with masks and vine trails. *Lunettes* with central half-pendants on cherub corbels, decorated with stiff hand- moulded thistles. N end lunette has a coat of arms (Farewell impaling Warde). *Frieze*, the same as Manor Farm nearby, grotesque with shields. Wing Chamber N end: *barrel ceiling*, thin-rib pattern, small central pendant. All *c*.1630. *(page 17; fig. 67)*

54 ■ **Manor Farm, Laverton**. Parlour: heavy single-rib *ceiling*, densely patterned with quatrefoils and thin-stemmed floral motifs. Two-tailed mermaid in square central panel, fishes in side panel. Grotesque well moulded *frieze* with shields, one dated 1627; gryphons, dogs, etc. from same mould as used in other houses in the Frome area and in Manor Cottages. *(page 16; fig. 68)*

LYDEARD ST LAWRENCE

55 ■ **Lower Tarr Farm**. Wing Chamber: *frieze*, grotesque foliate with deer and shields. *Overmantel*, two central winged horses with vase-pedestal between, initials R D E, dated 1691, and isolated deer and fleurs-de-lis. An anachronous design using early-style motifs.

MARSTON MAGNA

56 ■ **Wyndhams**. Wing Chamber: Pegasus *frieze* of winged horses, a narrower frieze than the one found nearby (Manor Farm, SOUTH BARROW, the only other Pegasus frieze found in Somerset). Other chambers: floral *friezes* of a simple serpentine pattern, seen in other houses, e.g. The Gables, STOKE SUB HAMDON. All early to mid C17. *(page 26; fig. 95)*

MARTOCK

57 ■ **Bower House, Bower Hinton** (formerly the Red Lion inn). Hall Chamber: on the sloping window soffit, a large *plaque* (possibly a former overmantel) nearly 8 ft. long, comprising a central strapwork roundel with date 1632 and initials I M P flanked by two winged female half-figures and large-scale foliated scrolls with monster heads, strongly reminiscent of the Chamber frieze in Whitestaunton Manor and perhaps by the same hand. *(fig. 125)*

58 ■ **Hurst, Bower Hinton**. Hall: soffit of bay window, a free foliated trail. (A modern copy above the fireplace).

MELLS

59 ■ **The Manor House**. E Parlour: a two-panel *ceiling* divided by a wide strip comprising two lines of flat frets, each panel with four large corner sprays of fruit and flowers, early to mid C17. W Parlour: a modern geometric *ceiling* in thin-rib with stiff hand-modelled sprays. (Another like ceiling is in Greenham Barton, STAWLEY, executed by Smallcorn of Bath and both designs are based on the ceiling in Merchant's Barton, Frome, the house now demolished).

MILVERTON

60 ■ **Bell House**, part of St Michael's House. Chamber: a three-sided *barrel ceiling*, thin-rib petal pattern with fleurs-de-lis and large rose paterae. *Lunette*, isolated fleurs-de-lis with two sprigs and leaf terminals, probably incomplete, late C16. *(fig. 55)*

61 ■ **Little Fort**. Wing Chamber: *lunette* to former barrel ceiling, a central plain shield in heavy strapwork frame, central mask and corner fleurs-de-lis, flanked by two unique rectangular panels with floral arabesques based on Crown Imperial flowers with acorns and leaves, *c*.1600. *(page 39; fig. 45)*

62 ■ **Lower Lovelynch Farm**. Parlour: *overmantel*, elaborate strapwork cartouche with leaping fish in central oval flanked by thin spirals of leaves and flowers, all in an enriched frame. Parlour Chamber: *overmantel*, similar strapwork cartouche with thin spirals, central oval and faded coat of arms supported by two hands grasping bows. Fireplace surround, enriched strips of floral meanders. Early to mid C17.

MONTACUTE

63 ■ *****Montacute House**. A great deal of plasterwork, all of similar date and of the highest quality, but no decorated ceilings. Hall: a narrow grotesque *frieze* with opposed dolphins (cf. the Hall frieze at Nettlecombe Court). High-end *wall panel*, filling the whole width of the hall, an animated *scene* in high relief, the 'Skimmington Ride', in which a hen-pecked husband is carried through the street on a pole; an unfeeling bucolic scene. Parlour: flat fret *frieze* with shields and animals. Dining Room: repositioned *overmantel*, Phelips coat of arms in cartouche dated 1599 surmounted by an C18 bust. Deep *friezes* occur in the Crimson Room (floral sprays) and Library (strapwork and flat fret). *Overmantels* in the same strapwork style, two with *scenes*, Judgement of Paris and King David praying to the Sun (God) (Psalm 84.11) and, in the Hall Chamber, a Phelips coat of arms flanked by male terms. All *c*.1600-10. *(page 17, 25, 26, 34, 42; fig. 1, 48, 97, 99, 104, 116)*

NETTLECOMBE

64 ■ **Huish Barton Farm**. Hall: a plaster *plaque*, high up on the brick end wall, a flowing monogram of G M for George Musgrave in William and Mary style ornate letters and the date 1698.

65 ■ **Nettlecombe Court**. A remarkable display of plasterwork spanning dates from *c*.1600 to *c*.1700. Hall: *ceiling*, partly enriched double-rib, three large pendants and many floral sprays, Jacobean style. Grotesque narrow *frieze* as in the Hall at Montacute. Huge *overmantel*, elaborate strapwork, rectangular central panel with achievement of arms and supporters (Trevelyan impaling Chichester); on the entablature six more shields, all early C17. Wing Dining Room: *ceiling*, four panels between moulded beams on acanthus brackets, each panel with double-rib geometric pattern enclosing a small wreath (as Gaulden Manor, TOLLAND). *Frieze*, between the brackets, large-scale stylised angular meander, a unique design. *Overmantel*, coat of arms, Trevelyan impaling Strode, in strapwork cartouche with initials M S and date 1641 (George Trevelyan married Margaret Strode in the 1630s). Wing Chamber over: *ceiling*, oval wreath enclosing Trevelyan crest, enriched ribs and corner panels with horses' heads. *Overmantel*, strapwork cartouche, more naturalistic than the one below, between acanthus brackets and coats of arms of Margaret Strode's parents (Strode impaling Wyndham), a transitional design, *c*.1640. SE Parlour, Study adjacent and Chamber over: *ceilings*, all *c*.1700, high relief naturalistic wreaths of husks, foliage, etc. Study: with central heavily-moulded putto in palm fronds. (cf Farm Estate, FIDDINGTON). *(page 17, 19, 21, 37; fig. 18, 22, 43, 72, 77, 83, 96)*

NORTH CADBURY

66 ■ **North Cadbury Court**. Staircase: *ceiling*, a large isolated pendant, early C20, modelled on the staircase pendant in Chelvey Court, Avon. Chamber: *ceiling*, thin-rib complicated curvilinear design with flat fret enrichments and bearded heads. The modelling is not of the C17 and suggests a later date, perhaps C19.

NORTH CURRY

67 ■ **Lower Knapp Farm**. Hall: fragment of an early to mid C17 *frieze*, a steep floral and foliated meander with fruit, much obscured.

NORTH PETHERTON

68 ■ **Impens Farm, North Newton**. Parlour: a *ceiling* with a central four-lobed design in thin-rib enclosing a cruciform star with small floral sprays and roundels with fat cheeked cherub faces. A *frieze*, a good deal obscured by paint, of wreaths enclosing alternately cherub faces and another unclear motif, the wreaths supported by angel figures with vases of flowers between. All late C17.

69 ■ **Newton House, North Newton**. NE Parlour: *ceiling*, a simple central four-lobed design in thin-rib enclosing a curved sided square with small floral sprays and central boss. Mid C17.

70 ■ **The Chantry, Rhode**. Parlour Chamber: above the fireplace, an isolated heart-shaped voluted *cartouche*, the date 1655 and initials I W for Jasper Woodhouse, who succeeded his father Jasper in 1654 (*V.C.H. Somerset*, vi. 290 and n.; monumental inscription in N. Petherton ch.).

OLD CLEEVE

71 ■ **Binham Farm**. Porch Chamber: *frieze*, flat frets. *Overmantel*, an animated *scene* between female caryatids, The Triumph of Time, with high relief figures and winged Time on a chariot drawn by stage (cf. Montacute House, The Skimmington Ride). Fireplace lintel moulded in leafy strapwork (same mould as in No 18 Fore Street, TAUNTON). All early C17. *(page 34, 43; fig. 39, 117)*

72 ■ **The Croft, Washford**. Hall: a good *frieze* in a very low room; large scale thin-stemmed spirals with flowers, fruit and a cherub, well preserved. Early C17. *(page 26; fig. 93)*

73 ■ **Leigh Barton Farm**. Disused Chamber, now in adjacent farm building, but built as a Roman Catholic chapel: grotesque *frieze*, damaged and part missing below flat part of a three-sided barrel; urns with floral arabesques, *c*.1630 (*V.C.H. Somerset*, v. 52).

OVER STOWEY

74 ■ **Parsonage Farm**. Chamber: a rustic *scene*, Adam and Eve, Adam holding the apple; colouring probably an addition. One corner of the plaque set at an angle under the sloping ceiling, early C17. *(page 35; fig. 103)*

PILTON

75 ■ **Manor House, West Compton**. Hall: *ceiling*, six simple panels between moulded beams, each with flat-moulded oval and four rosettes, one oval interrupted by staircase, late C17.

PITMINSTER

76 ■ **Poundisford Lodge**. Parlour: *ceiling*, thin-rib geometric with floral sprays. *Frieze*, anthemion alternately inverted with flat scrolls (cf. Marshwood Farm, CARHAMPTON). White Chamber and Oak Chamber: both with segmental *barrel ceilings*, thin-rib stellar pattern, the former with large central pendant. *Lunettes*, thin-rib squares with fleurs-de-lis, Tudor roses and coronets. *Friezes*, as ground floor. *Overmantels*; White Chamber: biblical *scene* in oval cartouche flanked by male caryatids on plinths with initials W S and E S (William and Elizabeth Symes). Oak Chamber: strapwork cartouche with date 1590 and initials W S and E S in central oval with flanking naked figures sitting on scrollwork (cf. Montacute House). All *c*.1590. *(page 7, 15, 25, 35, 42; fig. 7, 55, 60, 105)*

77 ■ **Poundisford Park**. Magnificent plasterwork of mid to late C16 and late C17. Thin-rib geometric *ceilings* in Hall (with many pendants), Screens Passage, Porches, Oriels, Gallery and principal Chambers, even second floor Chambers. Two Hall pendants have initials W H and L H for William Hill and his wife Lucy (nee Ryves). Their marriage *c*.1570 may date the plasterwork. All major rooms have grotesque *friezes*, the Hall frieze above a deeply coved cornice. The Gallery and King's Room friezes are from the same moulds as those used in Holcombe Court, Devon, and at Haddon Hall, Derbyshire. At the high end of the Hall a *wall panel*, the coloured arms of Elizabeth I enclosed in an enriched double-rib lozenge (the same moulds as in Rowlands, ASHILL). All *c*.1570. NW Parlour: *ceiling*, a central oval wreath enclosing the Hill crest (dove with olive branch), wide bands and corner panels with floral scrollwork, moulded cornice, *c*.1660. NW Chamber: small floral *frieze*, repeated in Gazebo, *c*.1700. *(page 15, 18, 23, 32; fig. 3, 55, 59, 73, 84, 85)*

RUISHTON

78 ■ **Musgrove House, Henlade**. Parlour: *ceiling*, four panels between beams with corner floral sprays and central motifs. Beams enriched with running pattern of leaves and fruit, *c*.1640.

SAMPFORD BRETT

79 ■ **No 7, Sampford Brett**. Parlour: *ceiling*, two panels divided by central beam, each with two unsophisticated decorations of stiff floral and leafy sprays with seeds and fruit, arranged like St Andrew's crosses. Each has initials in the small central medallion, E S, I S, I S, S W. One decoration has small faces in terminal leaves, a most unusual design, mid C17.

Selwood

80 ■ **The Grange**, **Tytherington**. Chamber: two-panel *ceiling* divided by beam, each panel with two large quatrefoils in single-rib, each enclosing a square and central Tudor rose with unusual floral sprays with monster heads, early C17, recently restored. (Same moulds used in No 3 Cork Street, FROME). *Wall plaque*, heart-shaped with chevron, dated 1661 with initials R B, probably for Robert Bisse, clothier (inf. from Michael McGarvie).

81 ■ **Rodden Manor**, **Rodden**. Parlour: *overmantel* in the form of a grotesque frieze (as in Laverton Manor Farm, LULLINGTON) with a central shield of arms of the a' Court family. Below the frieze a band of large-scale floral motifs. Date 1663 on house may date the plasterwork.

Shapwick

82 ■ **Forsters**. A medieval house. First-floor landing: *wall* decoration, three large fleurs-de-lis, another over the Solar doorway with the date 1712 and initials B T R, probably for members of the Bartlett family (Thomas Bartlett lived there in 1754: S.R.O., DD/SG 36). Solar: simple foliate *frieze* with stylised flowers (also at Wyndhams, MARSTON MAGNA). If of the early C18, then very old moulds were being used. *(page 26; fig. 10, 95)*

Somerton

83 ■ **Manor House**. Hall Chamber: *ceiling*, thin-rib geometric with petals in large squares and floral sprays, the pattern truncated one side by inserted partition. *Overmantel*, Dodington coat of arms in a lozenge with terminal fleurs-de-lis flanked by recessed panels supported on miniature decorative columns (identical to the double pedestals on the mid C16 overmantel at Mapperton, Dorset). All mid C16, some of the earliest plasterwork in the county. The house rebuilt mid C17, the plasterwork presumably a survival from an earlier house on the site (*V.C.H. Somerset*, iii. 132). *(page 15, 30; fig. 35)*

South Barrow

84 ■ **Manor Farm**. Chamber: *ceiling*, thin-rib petal pattern, all curves, with two types of floral spray, small flowers and central boss surrounded by small Tudor roses. Pattern does not go up to the edges of the room but forms a large central feature. Pegasus *frieze*, winged horses oppose one another above a floral mound with ribboned baton between (also at Stockton House, Wilts., and Forde House, Newton Abbot, Devon, *c*.1610). All early C17.

South Petherton

85 ■ **Old Bridge**. Hall: a long rectangular *overmantel*, formerly in Plainsfield Manor (now Court Farm), Over Stowey. Two Blake coats of arms with initials I B E for John and Elizabeth Blake (married 1662-3) and the date 1665, commemorating John's inheritance of Plainsfield. In the centre a panel of foliage scrolls (with pomegranates and fleurs-de-lis) around a lozenge with initials E B for Elizabeth Blake. It is virtually certain that the wife's initials would not have occupied the central position during her husband's lifetime, so it seems probable that the overmantel was erected after John's death in 1669. The use of the lozenge (for a widow) makes the suggestion more likely. The design is rather old-fashioned for the 1670s. (Blake family history from Mr W.S. Blake, South Petherton). *(fig. 108)*

86 ■ **Wigborough Manor**. Parlour: *ceiling*, thin-rib geometric with leaf bosses and many mythical animals, mermaid, man-at-arms, winged beasts, etc., (cf. animals at Weston Farm, WAMBROOK), all in very good condition (?restored). Deep *frieze*, flat strapwork with mask heads, rectangular cartouches with scenes (hunting and figures at a well); smaller frieze over windows. *Overmantel* below a very unusual cresting, a rectangular strapwork cartouche with coat of arms (Hele with Brome gauntlet impaling Compton below bird crest), flanked by primitive female terms with wimples, all *c*.1628, when Penelope (d. 1630), daughter of Brome Johnson, married Sir Thomas Hele (*V.C.H. Somerset*, iv. 178). Parlour Chamber: *ceiling*, plain thin-rib, all curves, no embellishments. Oriel and Oriel Chamber: *ceilings*, plain thin-rib geometric. All *c*.1590. *(page 17, 26, 31, 44; fig. 31, 50, 98, 100, 121)*

Spaxton

87 ■ **Gothelney Hall**. Hall: *ceiling*, divided by heavy axial beam into two panels of thin-rib stellar patterns with leaf bosses (recently coloured). The Hall ceiling continues over the Gallery but with a different geometric pattern, *c*.1600. Parlour: *ceiling*, thin-rib geometric with curves, floral sprays and unusual small foliate meander *frieze*, ? *c*.1700. Second floor Chamber: axial beam with large rosettes.

88 ■ **Stowey Cottage**. The only external plasterwork of note. Around windows and doorway facing the road, raised vine and oak trails now painted green against whitewashed stonework. Unorthodox and perhaps recent.

STAPLEGROVE

89 ■ **Yarde Farm**. Hall: *ceiling*, six panels between beams, each panel framed in plaster mouldings with large corner leaves, four isolated cherub heads and a central leaf boss. Parlour: *ceiling* with deeply coved cornice, a large bolection-moulded rectangular panel and a central plain oval. All late C17. *(fig. 54)*

STAWLEY

90 ■ **Greenham Barton**. Hall: C17 style modern *ceiling* by Smallcorn of Bath in enriched double-rib, the design like the Red Lodge, Bristol. Parlour and Parlour Chamber: Jacobean *ceilings*, petal patterns, thin-rib. Parlour: grotesque *frieze* (same mould as used for Great Chamber, Beckington Abbey, BECKINGTON) and a late C17 *overmantel* with isolated robust strapwork cartouche and coat of arms of the Bluett family, all in high relief, almost baroque.

91 ■ **Kittisford Barton**. Parlour: *overmantel*, large scale strapwork cartouche with shield of arms (Wood impaling Drake) and initials W and D. Drawing Room: concealed behind Georgian panelling an *overmantel* (or *frieze*) of four floral arches of what seems a continuous arcade of crude Jacobean pillars (cf. Hankridge Farm, WEST MONKTON). A portion of grotesque *frieze* survives above. The arcade may have extended across the room; *c.*1610. *(page 36)*

STOCKLAND BRISTOL

92 ■ **Rogers Farm**. Parlour Chamber: grotesque *frieze*, opposed snake-like dragons; simple rosettes in corners of *ceiling*. E Chamber: *wall plaque* dated 1675 and initials B R S.

STOCKLYNCH

93 ■ **Ilford Bridges Farm**. W-end Parlour, perhaps a Court Room: *ceiling*, divided by beams into three panels, centre panel a loose oval wreath of leaves with twisted stems, enclosing a shield of arms of the Speke family (double-headed eagle with boar crest) who owned the house; *c.*1690.

94 ■ **The Grove**. Two Chambers: a small *frieze* round all the walls and cross beam, a running strawberry meander of great charm and simplicity. Mid C17.

STOGUMBER

95 ■ ***Combe Sydenham**, **Monksilver**. W Wing 'Restoration Chamber': fragmentary C17 *frieze*. Ground-floor 'Court Room': has an enterprising modern barrel ceiling and frieze in the thin-rib Elizabethan manner by David Duncombe.

STOGURSEY

96 ■ **Cathanger Farm**. Parlour: six-panel framed *ceiling*, beams with small mouldings and wide plain chamfers decorated with alternate bird and flower motifs, probably C17. *(page 25)*

97 ■ **Steyning Manor**. Hall: impressive classical plasterwork. Three cross beams divide the *ceiling* into four plain panels, large acanthus leaf cornices around each panel. Big floral decorations in high relief on beam soffits. *Wall panels* over doors and windows with classical cherub heads and palm fronds, one with a raven. Dominating *overmantel*, classical design of leafy spirals and putti flanking central blank shield with large frowning masks above and below, all late C17. SW Parlour: *ceiling*, thin-rib interlocking petal pattern, small leaf bosses, *c.*1600. Parlour Chamber: *ceiling*, thin-rib central petal pattern with squares and circles containing Tudor roses and floral sprays. Hall Chamber: has occasional floral motifs on ceiling and walls. All early C17. Raven and Tudor roses both occur in the arms of the owning Burland family (*V.C.H.* Somerset, vi. 146). *(page 20, 37; fig. 111)*

STOKE SUB HAMDON

98 ■ **The Gables**. Hall: *ceiling*, thin-rib geometric with central petals, two types of floral spray and leaf bosses, *c.*1600 (possibly restored). Hall Chamber: good vine meander *frieze* with grapes and stylised flowers (cf. Wyndhams, MARSTON MAGNA, and Forsters, SHAPWICK). Early to mid C17. *(page 26; fig. 95)*

STRINGSTON

99 ■ **Plud Farm**. A wonderfully rich display of plasterwork in so small a house. Parlour: four-panel framed *ceiling* with deep chamfered beams, each panel with a different thin-rib pattern (one, the 'tulip' design from W. Gedde's book of 1615) with cast and hand-modelled flower motifs. A small shaped *wall* plaque with initials I P A for John Prior and his wife and the date 1622. Parlour Chamber: *overmantel*, one corner cut by sloping ceiling, with central *scene*, Abraham and Isaac (Gen. 22) flanked by female caryatids, Hope and Mercy, with strapwork surround above the same initials, I P, A P and the date 1641, all quite simply done. *Ceiling*, large elaborate corner sprays, c.1660 (cf. Chilton Trivet Farm, CANNINGTON). (*V.C.H. Somerset*, v. 92). *(page 15; fig. 17)*

100 ■ **Priors Farm**. A rich assembly of very naive design. Wing Parlour: *ceiling*, four panels between beams, each with scattered floral sprays. *Frieze*, primitive grotesque of almost dismembered vases and opposed dolphins taken along the sides of all the beams. *Overmantel*, wide rectangular panel with child-like 'pastry cook' plasterwork enclosing a shaped plaque with initials G P I, for George and Jane Prior, dated 1658. Parlour Chamber: shaped *wall plaque* with initials G P I dated 1641. Fireplace surround with running fruit and flower meander. (*V.C.H. Somerset*, vi. 174-5). *(page 25, 35; fig. 41, 46, 89)*

TAUNTON

101 ■ **No 18 Fore Street**. Great Chamber: enriched rib *ceiling*, stellar pattern with curves, stumpy central pendant and four shields of arms (Cornishe and Yonge). *Frieze*, thin-stemmed floral sprays in panels between enriched ribs to make a deep frieze (cf. Montacute House) with an upper narrow frieze of floral spirals and fruit above. *Overmantel*, *scene*, Abraham and Isaac (Gen. 22) in strapwork cartouche, flanked by female caryatids, Hope and Justice, c.1620. Ground floor back room: thin-rib geometric *ceiling* with floral sprays. *Frieze*, small section survives, as Great Chamber. Ground floor Wing room: beamed *ceiling* in sixteen panels, in each panel a central Tudor rose in a rectangular moulded frame. Remains of a deep *frieze*, as Great Chamber. All probably c.1600 in this fine town house associated with the Cornishe family. *(page 17, 44; fig. 51, 55, 120)*

THORNFALCON

102 ■ **Ashe Farm**. Chamber: *overmantel*, arcade of three floral arches in large rectangular frame of enriched ribs. Flower and leaf pattern in spandrels; bonneted, gnome-like figures (?mermaids) in floral arabesques under the arches, c.1610 (cf. Hankridge Farm, WEST MONKTON, but columns inverted). *(page 36; fig. 42)*

TOLLAND

103 ■ ***Gaulden Manor**. Fine transitional-style plasterwork, all c.1640 (*Proc. Som. Arch. Soc.* cxvi. 113-14). Hall: *ceiling*, early classical, one circular and two oval wreaths, the former with pendant, the latter enclosing low relief figures of the Last Trump and King David with his harp. All wreaths surrounded by residual strapwork and with plain connecting bands. Ornate floral deep *frieze* with scrolls and shields and small *scenes*. *Overmantel*, large strapwork design with four coats of arms flanked by double caryatids (two each side), Peace and Plenty. Mantelshelf supported on acanthus brackets with mask corbels. Parlour ('Chapel'): *ceiling*, four recessed and coved panels between beams, each with double-rib entwined geometric patterns (cf. Wing Chamber, Nettlecombe Court, 1641). Small floral meander on beams. *Frieze*, as Hall but mostly floral with putti. Between Hall and Parlour a suspended arcaded *screen* with pendants and cherubs in the spandrels and initials I T for John Turberville. Hall Chamber: *overmantel*, a well-executed achievement of arms with strapwork, fish-tailed bear supporters (crest and mantel cut off by ceiling): Turberville impaling Willoughby for marriage of John Turberville with Bridget Willoughby 1639. *(page 19, 27, 31; fig. 13, 20, 24, 29, 75, 101)*

TRULL

104 ■ **King's Gatchell**. Chamber: *overmantel* and part *lunette* to plain barrel ceiling, Royal coat of arms of James I with initials I R under a three-arch floral arcade flanked by large Tudor rose and fleurs-de-lis with crowns. Above, two winged angels; ends of the arcade supported on decorated inverted columns (cf. Hankridge Farm, WEST MONKTON, and Ashe Farm, THORNFALCON). Above the design the beginning of another floral arcade, only two arches remaining. All c.1610. *(page 36)*

WAMBROOK

105 ■ **Weston Farm**. Rich and exotic decorations in a farmhouse. Parlour: four-panel framed *ceiling*, each panel with a different double-rib design, three panels with Bonner and Compton arms (Henry Bonner married Mary Compton 1614: *Visitations of Somerset, 1623*, 10), all with many mythical beasts and real animals in realistic high

relief (cf. frieze in Whitestaunton Manor, c.1630). Parlour Chamber: flat soffit of three-sided barrel *ceiling*, covered all over with leafy thin spirals radiating from a central ring and, at each end, a stylised vase. A unique design for Somerset, but not unlike the more elaborate ceiling in Rashleigh Barton, Wembworthy, Devon. All c.1620. *(page 16, 17, 44; fig. 16, 64, 124)*

WAYFORD

106 ■ **Wayford Manor**. Parlour: *ceiling*, thin-rib geometric with some curves; leaf bosses, Tudor roses, fleurs-de-lis and floral sprays (possibly restored). The date 1602 on the stone overmantel in the same room may be right for the ceiling. Small Parlour: ceiling may be modern like the Hall ceiling, c.1900.

WEST BAGBOROUGH

107 ■ **Little Court**, formerly the Rectory. Solar: *lunette* to former barrel ceiling, a plain strapwork frame enclosing a flowering plant, flanked by large thin-stemmed spirals of leaves and pears. *Overmantel*, strapwork cartouche with achievement of arms of Kellett family, flanked by naked figures perched on scrolls, as in Combe Farm, WITHYCOMBE, 1629. (Edward Kellett rector from 1608 and still in 1641: *Somerset Incumbents*, ed. Weaver, 313; *Proc. Som. Arch. Soc.* lxxxiii. 126-7). *(page 26)*

WEST BUCKLAND

108 ■ **Buckland Farm**. Wing Parlour: four-panelled framed *ceiling*, each panel with square pattern of enriched double ribs, small floral sprays and central rose or oak-leaf motif; beam intersection with boss and four floral sprays, c.1620. Hall Chamber: *ceiling*, single-rib stellar pattern with curves and leaf bosses, c.1590.

WEST COKER

109 ■ **West Coker Manor**. Great Parlour Chamber: *overmantel* in strapwork with seated figures, fruit garlands and masks, similar to overmantels in Montacute House. Central coat of arms of Sir John Portman, c.1600. In the same room a *frieze* of alternately inverted tulips as in the Tudor Room, Gatehouse, COMBE FLOREY, dated 1593. Probably executed by Robert Eaton. *(page 42; fig. 8)*

WEST MONKTON

110 ■ **Hankridge Farm**. Hall Chamber: *overmantel*, in excellent condition; a rectangular enriched frame enclosing a three-arch floral arcade on tapering pillars (Ionic caps) above gnome-like figures (?mermaids) in symmetrical floral arabesques, with angels and female figures in the spandrels, c.1610 (cf. King's Gatchell, TRULL, and Ashe Farm, THORNFALCON). *(page 36; fig. 42)*

WEST PENNARD

111 ■ **Higher Southtown Farm**. Chamber: one of the two earliest *overmantels* found in Somerset (the other at the Manor House, SOMERTON). A good deal damaged and the left corner cut off by the sloping ceiling. A lozenge of decorated batons, identical to those at Mapperton, Dorset, enclosing a fleur-de-lis with three smaller ones outside, all flanked by two panelled pilasters with paterae. Mid C16. *(page 29; fig. 32)*

WHITESTAUNTON

112 ■ **Whitestaunton Manor**. Parlour: grotesque *frieze* with scrolls. First Floor Drawing Room: very remarkable *deep frieze* with coat of arms, Brett impaling White (Sir Robert Brett married Mary White c.1630: *Proc. Som. Arch. Soc.*, v. 82). A continuous trail of flat leaves and flowers with many non-repetitive large freely-modelled animals, mostly fabulous (cf. Court Room, CHARD, Wigborough Manor, SOUTH PETHERTON, and Weston Farm, WAMBROOK). In the same room an *overmantel* with a plain stiff strapwork cartouche containing the Brett arms and initials A B for one of the three generations of Alexander Bretts; perhaps c.1650. *(page 17, 26, 44; fig. 28, 122)*

WILLITON

113 ■ **Kentsford Farm**, Watchet, a Wyndham family farmhouse. Chamber: fine double-rib stellar patterned *ceiling* with interlocking ribs, floral sprays with roses and tulips and a central boss, early to mid C17.

114 ■ *Orchard Wyndham**. SE Solar: an early geometric thin-rib *ceiling* with Wyndham and Sydenham arms and large, well-moulded fleurs-de-lis, mid C16. NW Solar: thin-rib geometric *ceiling*, probably coeval with SE Solar, with vine leaf spirals and grapes in square bosses. Peacock Chamber: *ceiling*, replaced with timber ribs,

C19, plain thin-rib geometric. Unique, unconventional *frieze* with peacocks, cherubs, cockatrices, gnomes, etc., all in panels divided by symmetrical balusters and leaf patterns; a rich naive interpretation of classical motifs. Late C16. *(page 14, 24; fig. 10, 14, 26, 55, 87)*

WITHYCOMBE

115 ■ **Combe Farm**. Parlour: *overmantel* painted brown and cut off at the top. Central oval strapwork cartouche dated 1629 with initials G B, A B, I B, D R (not identified); naked flanking figures perched on strapwork scrolls, similar to Little Court, WEST BAGBOROUGH.

WIVELISCOMBE

116 ■ **Bournes**. Wing Parlour: *ceiling*, large central wreath of fruit and flowers with inner scrolly band enclosing two figures in relief, Cupid and Venus, and the motto SINE CERERE ET BACCHO FRIGET VENUS (without bread and wine (even) love grows cold); all very similar in style to the ovals at Gaulden Manor, TOLLAND. Remainder of ceiling divided by enriched laurel-leaf bands in rectangular patterns, mid C17. *(page 19; fig. 76)*

117 ■ **No 1 High Street**. Front Chamber: good late *ceiling*, c.1700, in two panels divided by plastered coved beam, one with free floral wreath, cherub heads in corners and semi-circular ends, shells and palm fronds; cornice enriched with flowers in high relief. The other panel is incomplete; floral wreaths in squares with leaf decorations in cornice.

118 ■ **West Braynes**. Wing Parlour: *ceiling*, early Georgian, plain oval broken into four spandrels with central flower, egg and dart mouldings. Classical cornice and pilasters beside fireplace. Early C18.

SOME PLASTERWORK IN ADJOINING COUNTIES

The selected examples have been added here partly for their intrinsic interest and partly for their relevance to work in Somerset.

BARROW GURNEY, Avon

Barrow Court. Some of the plasterwork, at first sight early C17, shows exotic characteristics that may be an outcome of proximity to the rich city of Bristol or may represent later work with antiquarian tendencies, perhaps of c.1700. In particular the fine, imaginatively-designed Staircase *ceiling*, in deep single-rib petals radiating from a central pendant is almost on the lines of Gothic tracery while the accompanying deep *frieze* has larger and fiercer dragons than any seen elsewhere. The fine Great Chamber *ceiling*, in thin-rib geometric pattern with birds and animals, is more clearly of the C17. The *overmantel* in the Parlour Chamber (Justice Room) comprises an achievement of the Gore arms flanked by huge, stout female caryatids, Justice and Mercy, all highly coloured like ships' figure-heads, c.1700. *(page 18; fig. 58, 74)*

BEAMINSTER, Dorset

Mapperton House. Great Chamber: *ceiling*, an elaborate thin-rib geometric design with many pendants, quite possibly the inspiration for the Hall ceiling at Poundisford Park, PITMINSTER. *Overmantels*, in the Library Chamber and the Drawing Room Chamber, comprise Italianate Tudor motifs, all very small in scale; decorated batons set lozenge-wise, decorated columnettes and roundels with renaissance heads, male and female, all of the 1540s to 1550s. Elements of these decorations (but not the roundels) are repeated in overmantels in the Manor House, SOMERTON, and in Higher Southtown Farm, WEST PENNARD, probably using the same moulds as at Mapperton. *(page 15, 23, 30; fig. 25, 33, 56)*

CHELVEY, Avon

Chelvey Court. Almost the only plasterwork decoration comprises one enormous isolated *pendant* above the Staircase, probably mid C17, with only minimal single-rib petals around it. One neat floral wreath occurs on the Parlour *ceiling*. *(page 18; fig. 19)*

CLAYHANGER, Devon

Nutcombe Manor. The Hall *ceiling* pattern is taken from W. Geddes's book of designs, published 1615. One of the panels in the Parlour *ceiling* of Plud Farm, STRINGSTON, is a smaller replica. *(page 15; fig. 61)*

Dartmouth, Devon

No 12 The Butterwalk. Chamber *ceiling*: Tree of Jesse in high relief forms an overall pattern of spirals, 1630s (cf. Rashleigh Barton, WEMBWORTHY). Either of these ceilings could have been the inspiration for the overall spirals on the Chamber ceiling in Weston Farm, WAMBROOK. *(page 16)*

Holcombe Rogus, Devon

Holcombe Court. Much fine plasterwork. The early Gallery *ceiling* comprises long chains of straight thin ribs with lozenges and the initials of Sir Roger Bluett (died 1566). *Friezes* in the Gallery and E Chamber are from the same moulds as used for the King's Chamber and Hall respectively in Poundisford Park, PITMINSTER. The Court Room at Holcombe has an *overmantel* dated 1591 with many design characteristics which link it with the overmantel in the Tudor Room in the Gatehouse, COMBE FLOREY, both probably by the craftsman Robert Eaton of Stogursey. *(page 15, 24, 42; fig. 115)*

Swimbridge, Devon

Dean Head. Chamber *overmantel*; Scene, 'The Triumph of Time' in a strapwork surround. (cf. **Binham Farm**, OLD CLEEVE). *(page 34, 43; fig. 118)*

Thorncombe, Dorset

*Forde Abbey. Magnificent early classical *ceilings* in Dining Room and Drawing Room (*c.*1655), ponderous and overwhelming, with wreaths and central ovals containing figures, heavy cornices and much scrollwork all in high relief. These ceilings preceded the more classically correct plasterwork in Dunster Castle, DUNSTER, and Halswell House, GOATHURST. *(page 8, 19, 45; fig. 9, 80)*

Wembworthy, Devon

Rashleigh Barton. Parlour *ceiling*, overall pattern of spirals with fruit, animals and flowers. See No 12, The Butterwalk, DARTMOUTH. *(page 16; fig. 17)*

**125. Bower House,
Bower Hinton, Martock**
*Chamber wall panel
(cf. the style of frieze at
Whitestanton Manor)*

GLOSSARY

PAGE REFERENCES indicate a fuller explanation in the text

Acanthus . . . .   The leaf of the plant used as a basis for classical ornamentation.

Acanthus bracket . . . .   A scrolled bracket of acanthus-leaf form.

Amorino . . . .   see **Putto**.

Anthemion . . . .   A stylised honeysuckle flower, ancient Greek in origin.

Arabesque . . . .   A pattern of flowing lines interwoven with leaves, flowers, etc., originally based on Moorish designs.

Architrave . . . .   The lowest member of the **entablature**.

Armature . . . .   The rigid framework of wood or metal around which to model plaster figures, foliage etc.

Badge . . . .   A small heraldic device, separate from the coat of arms.

Barrel ceiling . . . .   A tunnel-like form; segmental three-centred or three-sided, usually in a room under the roof.

Bolection moulding . . . . . .   A heavy S-shaped, projecting moulding used as a frame to late C17 door or fireplace openings, etc.

Boss . . . .   A decorated knob at the intersections of ceiling ribs.

Capital . . . .   The spreading decorated top of a column supporting the **entablature**.

Cartouche . . . .   A decorative plaque of any shape, often the centrepiece of an overmantel.

Caryatid . . . .   Used here to mean any full length figure standing either side of an overmantel *(page 49)*.

Chamber . . . .   Any upper room in a house.

Cherub . . . .   A disembodied angel face with one, two or three pairs of wings.

Chevron . . . .   An inverted V.

Closet . . . .   A small room, usually serving a larger **chamber**.

Cornice . . . .   The overhanging horizontal member at the top of the **entablature**.

Cornucopia . . . .   Horn of Plenty; a twisted horn overflowing with fruit, etc.

Cove . . . .   A concave overhang, usually as a **cornice**.

Egg and Dart . . . .   A classical decoration of ovals and triangles along a moulding.

Enrich(ment) . . . .   A pattern, usually applied as a running **meander** on double ceiling **ribs**.

Entablature . . . .   The whole of the horizontal member above the columns of a classical building, including **architrave**, **frieze** and **cornice**.

Fan Vault	A late Gothic vault with spreading, fan-like **ribs**, often with **pendants** in later work.
Finial	A decorative top-knot on a stair newel, roof gable, etc.
Flat Fret	A flattened two-dimensional version of **Strapwork**, like fretwork.
Floral Spray	A small spray of leaves and flowers usually decorating a ceiling.
Flutes	Grooves or raised ribs running up and down a column or vase.
Fret	A C16 and C17 term for a ceiling pattern.
Frieze	The middle member of the **entablature**, usually decorated.
Geometric	Description of a ceiling or other pattern, mostly of straight lines and right angles.
Grotesque	From Italian *Grotesche*, the basis of much of renaissance decoration *(page 6)*.
Guilloche	A classical decoration of interweaving circles.

Hall	Until about 1600 the most important room in the house.
Impale	To arrange two coats of arms side by side on a shield to display the arms of husband and wife.
Intaglio	Design cut in reverse, as on a mould or seal.
Ionic	The **order** of classical architecture with voluted **capitals**.

Key Pattern	Geometric pattern of intersecting or flowing waves.

Lath	A thin strip of wood.
Lintel	The horizontal beam or stone over an opening.
Lozenge	A square or rhombus set diagonally, in heraldry denoting a widow or spinster heiress.
Lunette	The semi-circular or trapezoidal end of a **barrel ceiled** room *(page 12, 14)*.
Meander	A running, repetitive curving wave pattern, usually of plant forms.

Mermaid	Half woman, half fish, allied to the Sirens of Homeric legend.
Modillion	One of a row of small, curly brackets under a classical **cornice**.
Mullion	A vertical stone or timber member dividing a window into two or more lights.
Newel	The post in the centre of a circular stair or at the angles of a rectangular one.
Order	One of the three principal systems of design of columns and **entablature** in classical architecture: Doric, **Ionic** and Corinthian.
Oriel	A small room off the high end of the medieval **Hall**, often for family dining.
Oriel Window	A projecting window, not necessarily lighting the **Oriel**.
Pargetting	The decoration of external plasterwork with raised or incised patterns.

Patera	A small circular ornament; in plasterwork sometimes treated as a flower.
Pediment	Triangular end of a low-pitched roof, also used decoratively in classical architecture over windows, doors, etc.
Pendant	Decorative hanging feature terminating in a small boss, to mark the nodal points of a ceiling **fret**. **Cage pendant**, the same but hollowed out *(page 18)*.
Pilaster	A flat half-column set against a wall.
Pulvinated	Pillow-shaped or convex, usually of a **frieze** or **architrave**.
Putto	An idealised naked infant; if with wings sometimes called an **Amorino**
Render	Coarse lime/sand plaster on a wall
Segmental	Formed from the arc of a circle of less than 180 degrees
Scroll	A decorative rolling spiral of leaves, **strapwork**, etc.; the rolled-up edge of a **strapwork** panel

Solar	The upstairs living room in a medieval house
Spandrel	The triangular space above and between adjacent arches or in the corners of an arch within a rectangular frame

Strapwork	An Elizabethan and Jacobean pattern of interweaving flat 'straps' *(page 8)*.
Swag	A drape of material (if of fruit and flowers, called a garland), used as a decoration on classical friezes, etc.

Term	A **caryatid** whose lower half is an architectural rectangular pedestal *(page 31)*.
Tracery	Decorative patterns of stonework in the upper part of an arched medieval window
Travertine	A hard Italian limestone from Tivoli
Wattle and Daub	Rough plaster made with earth on a wattle or basketwork support, used as an infill between wall timbers

BIBLIOGRAPHY

Bankart, G. P., *The Art of the Plasterer* (1908)

Beard, G. W., *Decorative Plasterwork in Great Britain* (1975)
   The English House Interior (1990)

Bush, R. J. E. 'Nettlecombe Court, the Trevelyans and other residents of the Court', *Field Studies*, vol. 3. no. 2
   (1970), 275-86.

Dunning, R. W., *Some Somerset Country Houses* (1991)

French, K. & C., 'The Frithelstock Book', *The Countryman*, liii, no. 4 (Winter 1956)
   'Devonshire Plasterwork' in *Transactions of the Devonshire Association*, 89 (1957), 124-44.

Gedde, W., *A Booke of Sundry Draughts* (1615)

Gerard, T., *The Particular Description of the County of Somerset* (Somerset Record Society xv (1900))

Hall, J., *Dictionary of Subjects and Symbols in Art* (1979)

Howard, M., *The Early Tudor Country House* (1987)

Jourdain, M., *English Decorative Plasterwork of the Renaissance* (1926)
   'A Seventeenth Century Plasterer, John Abbott of Barnstaple,', *Country Life*, 2 March 1940

Maxwell Lyte, H. C., *A History of Dunster*, (2 vols. 1909)

Oswald, A., *Country Houses of Dorset* (1935)
   'Montacute Re-visited, III', *Country Life* 3 Nov. 1955, 1022-3.

Pegg, B.F. and Stagg, W. D., *Plastering - a Craftsman's Encyclopedia* (1976)

Pevsner, N., *South and West Somerset* and *North Somerset and Bristol* (Buildings of England, 1958, reprinted
   1979)

Serlio, S., *The Five Books of Architecture* (1537; 1611 edn. reprinted 1982)

Somerset Incumbents, ed. F. W. Weaver (1889)

Stagg, W. D. and Masters, R., *Decorative Plasterwork - its repair and restoration* (1986)

The Somerset Protestation Returns and Lay Subsidy Rolls, 1641/2, transcribed A. J. Howard, ed. T. L. Stoate
   (1975)

Summerson, J., *Architecture in Britain, 1530-1830* (Pelican History of Art, 1953)

The Trevelyan Letters to 1840, ed. M. Siraut (Somerset Record Society lxxx (1990))

Thorp, J., 'Plasterwork', in *Devon Buildings*, ed. P. Beacham (1990)

Turner, L., *Decorative Plasterwork in Great Britain* (1927)

Victoria History of Somerset, ii, ed. W. Page (1911); iii--vi, ed. R. W. Dunning (1974, 1978, 1985, 1992)

The visitation of the county of Somerset in the year 1623, ed. F.T. Colby (Harleian Society, 1876)

Vivian-Neal, A. W., 'The Tudor and Stuart Plasterwork of West Somerset' in *Proceedings of the Somerset
   Archaeological and Natural History Society*, xcvi (1951), 143--51